WE
THE PEOPLE

STORIES FROM THE COMMUNITY RIGHTS
MOVEMENT IN THE UNITED STATES

Thomas Linzey and Anneke Campbell

PMPRESS

2016

We the People: Stories from the Community Rights Movement in the United States
© Thomas Linzey and Anneke Campbell 2016
This edition © 2016 by PM Press

ISBN: 978-1-62963-229-2
Library of Congress Control Number: 2016948140

Cover by John Yates/stealworks.com
Interior by Jonathan Rowland
All images courtesy of CELDF (celdf.org) and *We the People 2.0*
(wethepeople2.film).

10 9 8 7 6 5 4 3 2 1

PM Press
PO Box 23912
Oakland, CA 94623
www.pmpress.org

Printed in the USA by the Employee Owners of Thomson-Shore
in Dexter, Michigan.
www.thomsonshore.com

"*Never doubt that a small group of thoughtful, committed citizens can change the world. Indeed, it is the only thing that ever has.*"

—Margaret Mead

To Stacey, Ben, Emelyn, Mari, Kai, Brad, Chad, Tish, Michelle, and Shannon—the ones who went first, and to all of the municipal officials and community leaders who have taken the plunge with them.

In memory of Gail Darrell.

CONTENTS

Preface

IN THE PAGES THAT FOLLOW, YOU will meet people from all walks of life—men and women who have left their comfort zones to protect their communities from destruction, and who are now pushing for a new system of law that would guarantee all communities the power to make decisions about activities that affect them.

You will meet Gail Darrell from New Hampshire, who left her garden to stop water-bottling corporations from taking her town's water, and Michael Vacca, from western Pennsylvania, who poured concrete by day and tried to stop coal corporations from destroying his community by night. You will meet Cathy Miorelli, a local elected official and nurse who, at a diminutive five feet tall, fearlessly led her borough council in taking on some of the largest waste corporations in the state of Pennsylvania. You will meet Rick Evans, a labor organizer with the Laborers Union in Spokane, Washington, who is working with others to protect the constitutional rights of workers. And you will meet Cliff Willmeng and his mother, Merrily Mazza, who together protected their town, Lafayette, Colorado, from fracking by passing a Community Bill of Rights and who now head up the effort to amend the Colorado State Constitution.

If you met these people on the street, you wouldn't think twice about them. But if you were to meet them in city hall, in a town meeting, or in a public hearing, you would watch them transform into fighters for their community and advocates for the ability of communities to govern themselves.

These people not only know that the "we the people" of historical fame have the right to change the law when it no longer functions to protect our communities; they believe that we have a duty to do so. And they're willing to devote their lives to making that real.

It's been a great pleasure over the past fifteen years to work with these people. All have become colleagues, and many have become close friends. Most importantly, none of them waited for someone to give them permission to act in defense of their communities. In other words, none waited for an environmental group to come along and try to save their community, or for a state or federal agency to "do the right thing." On the other side of the coin, they refused to listen to anyone who told them there was nothing they could do to keep their communities from being destroyed.

They just did it. They did it because they had run out of hope that anyone else would.

And so they stood up and began reprogramming their local governments. They demanded that their elected officials find a new way to protect the rights of residents. In so doing, they transformed the members of their local governments from mere administrators of decisions handed down from above into the first wave of a movement toward sustainability through local self-governance.

That, of course, sounds complicated. But the people laying the groundwork for a broader movement would tell you that it's actually quite simple—that they're just bringing their local governments in line with the original sentiments laid out in the Declaration of Independence. And the one overriding principle from it that has been driven into every single state constitution is this: governments exist to protect the rights of people and communities, and when they stop doing so, they must be overhauled so that they do.

Giving up hope that someone else will do this for them has freed them to do whatever they need to do, which includes examining whether the system of law that currently exists in the United States—which systematically deprives communities of the authority to stop fracking, pipelines, factory farms, and coal mining—is really a democracy.

Giving up that hope has liberated them to take whatever steps they need to take—stopping corporate projects in their communities, declaring that ecosystems have rights of their own that can be defended by people, forcing their local elected officials to resign when they refuse to do the will of community majorities, and getting sued for challenging court decisions that elevate the "rights" of corporations over the rights of people, communities, and nature.

It's structural change they're after, because they've become convinced that nothing short of that kind of change will actually take their communities off the defensive and put them in a place where they control their own futures. In short, they do it because there's nothing left to lose anymore in their communities. The cost of doing nothing has become more expensive than the cost of acting.

Many of the people who appear in the pages ahead have now embarked on an extended journey—joining hands with others in their states to propose state and federal constitutional amendments recognizing a community right to self-government.

These people are convinced—from the things they've seen, heard, and experienced—that nothing short of a complete overhaul of our system of law and government will solve the problems they face in their communities. And the results of their battles will eventually determine the course of a much larger challenge: whether we will continue to allow others to destroy our communities and the planet, or whether we will somehow find a way to align our governance and law with the state of the world in ways that don't.

So as you head into the pages that follow, we hope that you go beyond merely cheering for these folks who have pioneered a different kind of activism. They are relying on you to do the same.

In the end, you'll hear them saying something quite simple: if your community is in the crosshairs of some corporation, it's time to give up on the hope that others will help you. Get on with doing the work that will save your community and the places that you love. In taking action, you will become part of a group that, joining with others, will create a movement that will be impossible to stop and will change the face of this country forever.

—Thomas Linzey
    March 23, 2016

Introduction

Thomas Linzey, the Community Environmental Legal Defense Fund, and the Democracy School

TWELVE YEARS AGO, I SAT AMONG three thousand environmental activists gathered together for the annual Bioneers conference—a pantheon of rainforest protectors, GMO opponents, the elite of bio-mimicry designers and green tech innovators, as well as indigenous leaders and overworked environmental justice advocates, all present to gain inspiration and energy to wage the good fight for another year. I had not heard of the Community Environmental Legal Defense Fund, nor its founder, Thomas Linzey, but two minutes into his speech, we were riveted. When he declared, "The only thing environmental regulation regulates is environmentalists," the audience cheered in recognition. "There never has been an environmental movement in America," he continued, "because movements drive rights into the Constitution, and rivers and cougars and ecosystems have no rights."

Nor do communities have rights. Our cheers were fueled by the frustration of activists who have watched as federal and state laws such as the Clean Air and Clean Water Acts, rather than prevent pollution, have actually legalized environmental harms by shifting focus away from the harms themselves to regulating how much destruction of nature is allowed. But I, along with many others, had been ignorant of the common cause at the root of so much damage to our habitat, which is a complex layering of laws that have removed communities' right to say no. Linzey explained that it's as if the abolitionists had tried to regulate the number of whiplashes that could be used on every plantation but never declared the practice of slavery itself illegal.

This powerful metaphor removed blinders from my vision. As a member of Thomas Linzey's audience, I was curious to understand how this inspirational speaker came to pioneer a whole new way of looking at the law and protecting communities. We initiated a conversation, which led to participation in the Democracy School, some writing and video work with the Community Environmental Legal Defense Fund, and eventually to the writing of this book.

Linzey grew up in Mobile, Alabama, surrounded by animals. Big tortoises crept underfoot and flying squirrels bounded overhead. His family raised baby raccoons and nursed back to health a blue jay, which liked to perch on his shoulder during breakfast. Today his parents might be called "wildlife rehabilitators"; he assumed everybody lived this way.

As a law student at Widener Law School in Pennsylvania, Linzey investigated corporate charters in relation to pollution. He found that all fifty states have statutes that allow the attorney general to revoke a corporate charter in the event of wrongdoing. He wrote an article arguing that this power of revocation could be used by citizens to hold corporations directly responsible for the damage they create. "I did this work," he says, "under the illusion that people were looking for new ways to be able to approach the corporate power structure, but I found that nobody was looking for a new direction."

In the spring of 1995, with his partner Stacey Schmader and his former law professor Brenda Sue Thornton, he created the Community Environmental Legal Defense Fund (CELDF). CELDF began to help people in various communities research and prepare permit appeals. By 1997, the majority of CELDF's clients were community groups fighting against something they didn't want—a factory farm, an incinerator, a new Walmart. As a nonprofit law firm, they never turned anyone down, and after a few lean years, CELDF became solvent when it was given a fat check by an opponent to a highway project in Virginia.

Construction of this highway meant blowing apart a mountain and wreaking havoc in the pristine and historic Ellett Valley. At the time, Linzey believed in the effectiveness of the National Environmental Policy Act (NEPA), a federal law established to "create and maintain conditions under which man and nature can exist in productive harmony." CELDF brought forth five lawsuits against the highway project and lost every ruling. He finally understood that while the NEPA requires environmental impact statements for any project using federal money, there is no accompanying legal requirement to select the least environmentally destructive course of action. He concluded: "The act is supposed to inform decision makers, yet it is not binding on the decision. So it's really just a pointless expenditure of money that gives people the illusion that our environment is being protected."

In 2001, Linzey and Schmader drove their twenty-four-foot mobile law-office RV all around rural Pennsylvania, providing free legal services to people with little resources. Even though they were successful in their appeals at an almost perfect rate, corporations would always just fix the legal holes revealed by the appeal and then be granted license to install whatever it was the particular community was fighting against. "So we got awards and funding," Linzey says, "we got accolades and looked wonderful on paper, but in the end, the communities were losing."

Then calls began to come in from local governments in rural Pennsylvania that were trying to stop factory hog farms from inundating their communities with economic and environmental harms. The hog farm corporations were taking advantage of a 1993 state law, the Nutrient Management Act, which effectively nullified the local manure-management ordinances of over four hundred communities. Instead of assisting these communities to file the expected-to-fail permit appeals, CELDF decided to instead work with them to pioneer another approach—one focused on asserting the right of local community members to define the type of agriculture they wanted within their community. Linzey explains: "Regulatory programs are drafted by the corporations that benefit from them. It's the agribusiness corporations that control the regulatory framework of factory farms coming in, so we're faced with a system of laws, and it took us six years to truly understand that this is a *system* of law—which allows a board of directors to have more rights than five thousand people in the community."

Following the lead of nine midwestern states, CELDF began to draft local ordinances prohibiting agribusiness corporations from "engaging in farming" within a municipality. This represented the first effort at changing the focus from merely regulating environmental harms to subordinating corporations to local community control. Tiny rural Wells Township in Fulton County became the first municipality to adopt such an ordinance, with five other townships in the county following over the next year.

Linzey found himself spending more and more time on the phone with people who wanted to know if what CELDF was doing could be replicated in their own municipality. During one conversation, the caller

suggested that they start a school. In the spring of 2003, Linzey and colleagues taught the first "Daniel Pennock Democracy School," so named in
honor of Danny Pennock, a teenager from Berks County, Pennsylvania,
who died of sludge poisoning.

The Democracy School examines the way the U.S. Constitution was
written, how it was anchored in an English structure of law, and how the
Supreme Court has slowly interpreted it to enshrine the rights of corporations into settled law. The school explores a number of those judicial
interpretations, which have led to the Bill of Rights protecting corporations from the public.

Like many participants in the Democracy School, I already knew
that corporations had been given personhood rights, and that this was
why the *Citizens United* decision invalidated federal campaign finance laws
as violating the corporate "right" to free speech as a "person." I did not
know how this came about, that the Fourteenth Amendment to the U.S.
Constitution—the due process/equal protection amendment passed to
guarantee the rights of recently freed slaves following the Civil War—was
newly applied to protect railroad corporations. In *Santa Clara County v.
Southern Pacific Railroad* the Supreme Court formally bestowed crucial
constitutional human rights onto an entity of property.

I was astounded to learn not only that the court had applied Bill of
Rights protections to these legal entities called corporations, but that the
Commerce and Contracts Clauses of the U.S. Constitution have also been
interpreted and used by courts to strengthen and codify corporate rights
into law. For example, in *Dartmouth College v. Woodward*, in 1819, the
Supreme Court ruled that the state may not unilaterally alter any charter
issued to create a corporation, in effect making the state subservient to
business interests.

Participants in the Democracy School come to understand why the
inhabitants of a particular community cannot simply ban a particular
activity such as fracking. And it explained to me how I could witness in
one town an entire community rise up to pressure their representatives
to vote against a uranium mine, only to find out that this "democratic"
process was a charade because their representatives had no power to deny
the corporate permit. In addition, it becomes clear that because nature is
legally considered property, all environmental laws owe their existence to
congressional authority exercised through the Constitution's Commerce

Clause, thereby framing all action to protect nature as a commercial inter-action. This is why Superfund cleanup costs, for instance, end up being considered part of our Gross Domestic Product.

The Democracy School does more than deliver the bad news, how-ever. It also explores how equal rights movements have altered the law and driven new rights into the U.S. Constitution. There is a lot to be learned from the suffrage and abolitionist movements, which had to fight not only settled law but also the cultural belief in slavery and women's subservience as God's Will. The lesser-known populist and labor movements also have lessons for activists today. In the school's final sessions, people discuss how they can integrate rights-based organizing into a plan or campaign that addresses the issues of their particular locality. These issues are reframed so that, instead of fighting against a particular harm, participants are asked to describe what they are fighting for, and to create a vision of the community they want to bring into existence.

"Today," Linzey says, "it is our communities and natural systems that are treated as property under the law—just as slaves once were—because what's in our communities is routinely bought, sold, and traded without a whisker of local control. In many ways, this work walks in the footsteps of prior movements to transform ourselves from being property under the law to becoming people who harness the power of government to defend and enforce our rights."

When the school is completed and the participants return home, CELDF assists them in drafting local laws aimed at achieving their goals for their community and helps community leaders to adopt those laws. When the community members succeed in passing those laws, they are manifesting new rights for themselves through lawmaking at the local level. They are also committing a form of legal civil disobedience. In so doing, they have learned from prior citizens' movements that have openly challenged and then changed unjust laws, and believe today's dire threats to our common home demand no less from us.

For some communities, passing the law ends the threat of the unwanted project. For others it's only the beginning and is followed by the task of supporting the laws and their representatives against lawsuits brought by corporations or state agencies. In those cases, CELDF has stepped in and worked together with local attorneys to defend the com-munities and their ordinances.

It's important for activists to remember that opposition from corporations and government does not represent a failure of organizing but a necessary stage of its expression. Opposition makes the stakes clear to people who may still harbor the illusion of safety and control. Powerful as they are, and destructive as they can be, corporate entities maintain their entitlement in some part because citizens doubt that they can govern themselves.

Over the years, and since the first version of this book (*Be the Change: How to Get What You Want in Your Community*), CELDF's work has evolved and expanded in a number of ways. Many more communities are engaged in passing local laws, and in some cases lawsuits have ensued. This in turn is adding fuel to the call for community rights across the country. In five states there are now networks organizing to build a movement to enshrine community rights and rights for nature in the national consciousness and federal Constitution.

What follows in these pages is a collection of individual and community stories that can serve as a guide for both concerned residents and experienced activists looking for a new strategy. This form of organizing is unique in defying the usual red state/blue state or liberal versus conservative delineations, and brings people together to defend their communities and the ecosystems in which they are embedded. Each chapter embodies lessons that these communities learned through trial and error on the front lines, sometimes fighting for their homes and health and safety, other times stepping away from their own concerns to fight for the rights of their fellow creatures in our shared planetary home.

As you look through this book, you may not find the exact threat you face, or a law spelled out that fits your community's particular situation. The principles expressed, however, are the same for all communities. While changing long-settled governmental structures and laws may seem daunting, I invite you to be inspired by the courage and perseverance of those who came before, and those on the frontlines now, motivated by the profound knowledge that if we don't act, we may not have anything left to protect.

—Anneke Campbell
March 21, 2016

Chapter 1
Blaine and Grant Townships, Pennsylvania: The Illusion of Democracy

THE HISTORY OF OUR PROGRESS AS a people has always involved unhappy people coming together to improve their lives. Over the years this organizing has taken many forms in pressuring our government to expand citizens' rights and protections, but not all modes of organizing work for all conditions and times. Therefore, when working to create change, organizers need to continually evaluate whether their current approach is effective. An approach that has worked well in the past might now be outdated or ineffective, but this is not necessarily easy to recognize or admit. So it is with our system of environmental law and protection, which is shrouded in a belief in both its effectiveness and its excellence. In order to create true change, citizens must learn to recognize the complex structure of laws and governance that buffers corporations, entities that often control the decisions affecting an overall community.

It's not easy to question the prevailing belief that we live in a democracy. *Webster's Dictionary* defines a democracy as a form of government in which the supreme power is vested in the people and exercised directly by them or by their elected agents; it also states that in a democratic state, decisions are made by the common people, as distinguished from any privileged class. What the people in Blaine Township, Pennsylvania, came to realize was that one such "privileged class"—in this case, a mining company's board of directors—had more power to decide what happened in the community than did its own residents.

Blaine Township versus the Coal Companies
Blaine Township is a small rural township about forty-five miles southwest of Pittsburgh, in Washington County. The racial makeup of the township

is overwhelmingly white, and the majority of people live in Taylorstown, a one-stop-sign town. There are a total of twenty-two square miles within the municipality. Blaine is crossed by Buffalo Creek, a high-quality perennial stream that flows into West Virginia and dumps into the Ohio River. Its banks are scented by wildflowers and pervaded by the sounds of crickets and cicadas, and spanning the creek is the historic Saw Hill covered bridge. The township is a haven to sportsmen of all stripes—fishers, birders, people who come to train their dogs for hunting—and this provides a major source of income for the community.

Western Pennsylvania has been mining coal for 250 years, but no mining had ever occurred in Blaine, and its residents and township supervisors aimed to keep it that way.

Longwall Mining Approaches Blaine

The Pittsburgh coal seam, of which the Buffalo Reserve is a part, lies directly beneath Blaine. Coal companies purchased the rights to this coal a hundred years ago, putting the decision to early residents like this: "We're going to give you money for something we're probably not going to come for in your lifetime." In a poor county, few passed up an offer like that.

In 2003, Blaine Township resident and planning board member Michael Vacca became aware that the Consol Energy Company wanted to mine in Blaine when neighboring communities were experiencing one of the newest trends in coal removal: longwall coal mining. The procedure for longwall coal mining goes something like this: six to eight hundred feet below the earth's surface, depending on the seam, a machine moves across the face of the coal, grinding it up at tremendous speed. After the machines come through and remove the coal, the earth drops three to six feet above the seam. This is called subsidence. The damage created by subsidence has caused the practice of longwall mining to be banned in Germany—the country where it originated.

Muscular, with long sandy hair and a goatee, Michael Vacca looks like he might have stepped out of a book about the Wild West. He pours cement for a living and does not call himself an activist or an environmentalist, even though much of his time has been spent organizing both his own as well as surrounding communities in order to protect and conserve nature. He's knowledgeable and practical. When he bought his house thirty years ago, he planted trees to shelter the place from sun, wind, and snow.

Vacca saw that longwall mining was leaving communities decimated in its wake—aquifers dewatered, streams and rivers destroyed, historic buildings sunk into the ground, and local wells replaced with gray plastic tanks of water called water buffaloes, which squat like big gray lumps in a yard. Some people in Blaine had relatives or friends whose communities had been mined and the lands devastated, and who were then left to deal with the consequences.

Vacca cares deeply about the place that supports his life. He knows the Buffalo Creek watershed is the last contiguous forested flood plain in Washington County, as well as a critical habitat for neo-tropical migrating birds. The pristine watershed is home to many creatures that only breed in high-quality water—certain salamanders, for instance. There is no public water in the county, so everyone draws water from the ground. Pennsylvania's Clean Streams Act states that nobody may destroy a water source or not restore a stream to its original state. But a lot of times the only means of "restoration" involves pouring concrete, which means that mosses and ponds—the basis of stream life and habitat—are lost. Other times, "restoration" means running a pipe from one stream into another, which does nothing for a stream whose headwaters have already been destroyed. Clearly, the law doesn't work to protect the streams in actuality.

Michael Vacca spent months researching the harmful effects of longwall mining, learning that, during the 1990s, the state of Pennsylvania changed the state laws so that subsidence was built into mining permits, making it legal. In this area, as they say, coal is king.

MICHAEL VACCA: Coalfield environmental-activist groups advised us to appeal the permits issued by the Department of Environmental Protection to at least get a better deal on oil, gas, and coal leases. It seemed we had no choice in the matter, and that the only thing we could do was try to make the incursion of longwall mining as noninvasive as possible. I knew from my own past experience that this too was going to fail.

Previous Environmental Threats to Community

In 1999, Allegheny Power wanted to build a power plant in the beautiful valley just down the road from Saw Hill Bridge. Residents found out about the plan when the county lifted the covered bridge off its moorings and placed steel beams underneath it, so that it would be ready to carry truck traffic and construction workers. Later, they discovered that both their county and state agencies had known about the project for years (state legislators had continually courted mining lobbyists) but did not give them any notice. The energy generated by the plant would not service local communities, but instead would be sold to whoever would pay the highest price.

Vacca formed a group to fight the power plant through the regulatory system—in this instance, the Department of Environmental Protection. Since this agency issues permits, it soon became clear that there was little protection and much "permitting." Nevertheless, Vacca and friends raised funds and engaged an attorney and biologists to study the area. They applied for designation as an Important Bird Area with the Audubon Society. An archeologist was asked to research whether Williamson Station could be placed on a list of historic sites.

The group went through several rounds at different courts, petitioning and repetitioning, losing again and again. After all their efforts, they were not even allowed to introduce environmental impact studies in their case. Then they got lucky. The energy market suddenly stopped its expansion, and Allegheny Power decided to sell the land to the game commission. In order to prevent similar threats from arising in the future, Vacca decided to become a member of the town planning commission. To his chagrin, he discovered that Pennsylvania state municipal code required communities to make an allowance for any kind of commercial development.

MICHAEL VACCA: I discovered that we cannot say no. Since most of the subsurface mineral rights had already been bought, they were done deals from a lease standpoint. The best the other townships could do was to raise the fees or to try to get a higher price. But to me, this place is priceless.

Another local resident with a home she considers priceless is Karen Duerr, an attractive young woman with brown eyes that exude calm. Duerr has lived all of her twenty-seven years in an old brick farmhouse with a lovely front porch and a number of outbuildings, including an ancient silo. Her property is bordered on one edge by Buffalo Creek. Karen and her family grow and harvest hay, part of which they keep for their own animals, selling the rest to local farmers.

Like many other brick houses in the area, Karen's home has an old foundation, which doesn't take well to subsidence. She knows that if longwall mining takes place, the foundation of her home will most likely crumble. She also knows that longwall mining will compromise the area's water supply and destroy her beloved Buffalo Creek. As a little girl, Karen was always down at the creek; when it got dark outside, her parents knew where to find her.

KAREN DUERR: I love this place. I've lived here my whole life. My parents live here. This is my home and I don't want to see it destroyed.

Karen's father grew up in heavily polluted Pittsburgh, but he always dreamed of being a farmer. After he bought land in Blaine Township, he became a township supervisor, working to make conservation a reality. This brought him into battle with the Pennzoil Company, which owns the rights to the oil under many farms in Blaine. The company reopened two old oil wells on the Duerr family property, its right-of-way putting a driveway right through the pasture. Although Karen's father and others spent much of the mid-1980s raising money and meeting time and time again to fight against oil drilling, they could never prove substantively that Pennzoil was responsible for the erosion of their topsoil or the contamination of their water by petroleum leaks. The burden of proof required constant and expensive testing by scientists. And while contamination by Pennzoil was finally demonstrated, the company had on staff full-time lawyers whose job consisted of throwing doubt on the findings and claiming that it was the company, and not the community, which was facing discrimination.

KAREN DUERR: At the time, of course, I didn't know what the basis was that these corporations kept winning on. I was tired of complaining about it and wanted to do something, but I didn't know what. Then Michael Vacca came over and invited us to attend a Democracy School. I was cynical at that point, but I trusted Michael.

Group Turns to CELDF to Help Fight Assault

In his work on the planning board, Michael Vacca had started to update and upgrade the Blaine Township zoning ordinance. He figured that if he couldn't stop mining, he could at least try to minimize the damage. He was looking for the most restrictive language that would pass legal muster when someone referred him to the Community Environmental Legal Defense Fund (CELDF). Looking for advice, Vacca had a long talk with Thomas Linzey.

After Vacca explained the apparent rigging of the regulatory system against local communities, Linzey asked him a question: "If the regulatory and land-use laws can't stop the mining, are you willing to try something different?"

Linzey offered to hold a Democracy School in Blaine, explaining that the community needed to get educated about the current realities of democracy and self-governance. Vacca made a list of people he thought should attend, including farmers and local government officials. One of the people he connected with was Fred Cramer.

FRED CRAMER: My home is 156 years old. It will be destroyed if it is mined. I will lose everything I came to Blaine Township for: my quality of life, my retirement, my life savings, everything. And Blaine Township will lose its emergency water supply, which is my pond. I wanted to find out: Why don't we have a say in what happens here?

Group Identifies Root Cause of Problem

The three-day Democracy School, held in 2005, was an eye-opener for all who attended. They learned about how thirty-nine white men of property wrote the U.S. Constitution behind closed doors and made sure to represent their interests in the document at the expense of the rights and interests of 90 percent of the people. In fact, rather than trusting people to self-govern, many of our founding fathers didn't trust the people, believing, as Alexander Hamilton did, that a monarchical form of government was the best form of government.

On the second day of the school, participants delved into how judicial interpretations have led to the establishing of corporate "personhood," which has ultimately resulted in the Bill of Rights protecting corporations from the will of the people.

KAREN DUERR: When I attended Democracy School, I learned a lot that I didn't learn during my years of education. I didn't know that corporations are considered persons in the eyes of the law.

While corporations possess the same rights under the U.S. Constitution as ordinary citizens, they are not legally bound to respect people's constitutional rights. *This is so because constitutional rights were written to shield people from invasive governmental action (e.g., the First Amendment, "Congress shall pass no law . . ."), not corporate action. But because corporate decision makers are not governmental officials, corporations cannot be sued for violating a person's constitutional rights.*

Blaine Township's three supervisors attended the school. Scott Weiss, the chairman, is the manager of a testing company. He has lived in Blaine Township for thirty years.

SCOTT WEISS: It is shocking that corporations are seen as people. They're using our own amendments against us.

Another supervisor, Darlene Dutton, saw how she had been devalued as a human being in relation to corporations. Participants in the Democracy School also learned about the U.S. Constitution's Commerce Clause, and how it is applied today. Communities are not allowed to inhibit commerce, and just about anything can be defined as commerce. The Commerce Clause enables corporations to sue local and state governments when those governments adopt laws seeking to control or regulate commerce. This structure of law prevents people from implementing their visions of environmentally and economically sustainable communities.

Group Decides on New Rights-Based Course of Organizing

Something communities under this kind of threat or assault have in common is that they come together in reaction to a specific issue. They spend all their energies pushing against what they don't want, rather than asking themselves what they do want. In Democracy School, the conversation shifts so that people begin to ask: What kind of community do we want to live in? And what are we going to do to bring our vision for our community into being? The Blaine residents returned over and over to their main concern: Who decides what happens in Blaine?

The Blaine Township supervisors are responsible not only for the fiscal operations of the township, the township roads, and maintaining order, but also for following and maintaining a community vision. Considering the area's state game lands, these supervisors want their community to promote outdoor activities. They have a freshwater creek, some old-growth forest, an aviary, and a lot of wildlife. This is exactly the type of community they want to maintain. When they each became a supervisor, they took an oath to look after the welfare of the township and its people.

When the coal company started encroaching in the surrounding communities, the Blaine supervisors knew it was just a matter of time until their community was encroached on as well. At one time, Darlene Dutton used to think that mining could be regulated and controlled. Then she started seeing evidence all around her to the contrary. She soon realized you "get what you try to regulate."

The supervisors in Blaine noticed the majority of people in other communities didn't get motivated until they had already lost what they held dear. As elected representatives, they realized they had to have the foresight to protect their community. They decided to be proactive to prevent the loss of property, water, and habitat. And to do that, they knew they had to think innovatively.

MICHAEL VACCA: We had sample ordinances from CELDF. We examined the language contained in them. We were asking real, specific questions. What we liked about these ordinances was that they gave the power to the people. They are rights-based. Those of us who live and pay taxes here would be exercising our right to decide.

Group Codifies New Vision into Laws or Legal Structures

The township supervisors brainstormed and asked Thomas Linzey to write an ordinance banning longwall mining. The language came from all who were present during the discussions. Basically, the ordinance states that to protect the health, safety, and general welfare of the township, no corporation has the right to come and mine within township boundaries, or to harm the ecosystem within it.

Representatives Support New Structures

Once the supervisors unanimously approved the ordinance, it needed to be advertised, and then a time set for public comment. Michael Vacca, Karen Duerr, and other active Blaine residents went to all the meetings and spread the word further in the township. A lot of people got involved after being personally contacted and invited to the meetings. Blaine residents asked whether something similar had been done in other communities, and CELDF provided information about townships that had passed similar kinds of ordinances with success. Some Pennsylvania communities, for instance, had banned corporate sludge dumping, and not one ounce of sludge had been spread on the land.

The Ordinance's Introduction:

> An ordinance to protect the health, safety, and general welfare of
> the citizens and natural environment of Blaine Township by ban-

ning corporations from engaging in mining within the township; by banning corporate ownership of land and mineral estates used for mining within the township; by banning persons from using corporations to engage in mining; by banning the exercise of certain powers by mining corporations; by recognizing the rights of ecosystems and natural communities and by providing for enforcement of those rights.

At the meeting for public comment, most people judged the new ordinance a good thing. Many were thankful that the supervisors were standing up for the environment. They were also concerned about infrastructure problems, as they had paid good money for their wells and septic systems. Only two people spoke against the ordinance—a representative from the coal company and an attorney, who threatened the supervisors with lawsuits. The supervisors had to prepare themselves, not only for a possible suit against the township, but also that they could be sued personally. The support CELDF offered was reassuring.

SCOTT WEISS: It helps that we are united and have a lot of respect for each other. We're not going to let them divide us.

Community Passes Ordinance into Local Law

In October 2006, the supervisors unanimously passed the ordinance. Then, realizing that it was susceptible to corporate legal arguments if it came to a challenge, they passed a second ordinance stripping corporations of the right to be considered persons. In essence, they removed legal powers and privileges from corporations at the municipal level, creating a protective barrier for the community against the threat of coal mining.

In return, the coal company made a variety of efforts to curry favor in the region, including building a ballpark and bombarding the community with advertisements offering the promise of "clean" coal. Children brought home coloring books donated to the school from the coal company. These showed Frosty the Snowman with coal eyes and a father and mother thanking the coal company for electricity. It introduced the kids to all the terms used in mining and how it powers their video games.

Supervisor Scott Weiss deplored the propaganda because it made the real conversation democracy requires even more difficult. The community supervisors were accused by the coal company of standing in the path of progress and energy. But the supervisors were clear on this point: A corporation's ability to make a profit from a coal mine does not give it the right to ruin a community.

MICHAEL VACCA: In the end, you have to call it like it is. Are we going to prostitute ourselves? For what are we willing to sell ourselves, our land, our water?

Group Expands Education and Deepens Commitment

Once the ordinance passed, the next phase of the work began.

Michael Vacca and local residents formed the Buffalo Creek Conservation Association. Their hope was that communities facing the same threat would be willing to empower themselves by passing ordinances of their own, which would in turn strengthen the entire region. They sent letters to the other townships in Washington County, explaining how longwall mining works, telling them that it was coming to their area, and describing the Blaine ordinance. Vacca attended twenty-two township meetings to discuss the ordinance but there were few takers. People have a classic response: you can't win, this is the way it's been, this is the way it's going to be, don't ask me to help. That is a very significant ball and chain to dislodge.

The media often presents another obstacle in the attempt to create change. Mainstream media, which usually operates under the assumption that "progress" is necessary and good, often does not inform the public of their rights or allow for healthy debate. Instead it puts up a screen of propaganda, forcing people to take time to educate themselves—if they take any time at all.

Yet another obstacle to change is the threat of losing jobs. Coal companies have long used the threat of job loss to pit labor against environmental protection. But the reality is that the number of jobs in the coal industry has fallen by half due to mechanization. And longwall mining will take away other, more sustainable jobs, like farming. In the end, however, this is not about stopping mining, it's about who gets to decide.

KAREN DUERR: It's about our voice. Democracy means having a voice in the decisions that affect you. We know there's going to be a fight, and that we're going to go to court. And if we stand up and win some of these cases, then we'll have a precedent.

In order for organizing to be successful, a critical mass has to occur, which means that a majority of people in a community has to stand behind the effort to pass new laws. These new laws challenge local and state governments in ways they have never before been challenged. At some point during the fight, it becomes clear that, contrary to all they have been taught, everyday citizens do not have the right to self-government. That in itself will be a hugely educational moment—one to vaporize illusions in the struggle for a real, live democracy.

MICHAEL VACCA: This is the stuff the American Revolution left unfinished.

In Memoriam Blaine Township Ordinance

In 2008, six months after the adoption of the ordinance, two coal corporations filed a lawsuit contending that the anti-corporate mining ordinance adopted by the Blaine Township supervisors violated the corporations' constitutional rights under the First, Fourth, Fifth, and Fourteenth Amendments, as well as rights guaranteed by the Constitution's Commerce and Contracts Clauses. The coal corporations also claimed that the ordinance was preempted by Pennsylvania state mining laws. They demanded that a federal court nullify the ordinance, and that the court award monetary damage and attorneys' fees against Blaine Township, thus illustrating for all to see their indifference to the rights and the lives of Blaine residents.

Thomas Linzey and Ben Price, the local CELDF organizer on the ground in Pennsylvania, were ready and willing to go to court on behalf of the township. In order to strengthen Blaine's residents' power to defend themselves, they also started mounting a campaign to change Blaine from a municipal second-class township to a home rule municipality (see Grant Township below).

But as the reality set in for Blaine Township residents and their representatives, they realized it would be up to the courts to change settled law, and that legislators were unlikely to change the law as long as they were beholden to big coal. Up against the piles of money the coal company poured into their legal assault on the tiny township, and up against the fears of being embroiled in litigation for many years, the supervisors decided to rescind the ordinance.

Discouragement followed and the local organizing fell apart. The attempt to become a home rule township faltered, and a coal industry person ran for and was elected as a town supervisor, gradually poisoning the atmosphere for moving forward in any way. At the same time, Washington County was beginning to experience a different but equally pernicious form of drilling for fossil fuels. If longwall mining has not devastated the homes and environment of Blaine, it's because coal is giving way to the boom in natural gas produced by the new technology called horizontal hydraulic fracturing, or "fracking." Ironically then, big coal has found its nemesis, not in democratic decision making, but in its inability to compete with the cheaper cost of gas.

Grant Township Makes History

Situated on the other side of Pittsburgh, and with not many more residents than Blaine, Grant Township made history by doing what the people of Blaine had attempted—defending a lawsuit brought by an energy corporation and adopting the first rights-based municipal constitution in the country for their township.

On November 3rd, 2015, Grant residents voted-in their municipal home rule charter, which contains a local bill of rights, with 68 percent of the vote. This municipal charter is the community's response to the same kind of legal assault that accompanied the environmental threat to Blaine Township. The local bill of rights codifies environmental and democratic rights, and bans frack wastewater injection wells as a violation of those rights. (See Appendix.) While over a hundred other communities have amended existing charters with rights-based provisions, Grant Township's charter is the first that is written entirely on the basis of asserting and protecting rights.

In early 2014, Pennsylvania General Energy Company, LLC, proposed a hydraulic fracturing wastewater injection well for the community, for the disposal of oil and gas waste generated from hydro-fracking for natural gas. This went against the wishes of many of the township's residents, among them Stacy Long, a graphic designer in her mid-forties, and her parents and neighbors, who all love their unspoiled and unabashedly rural neck of the woods that goes by the name of "East Run," located in central Grant Township northeast of Pittsburgh.

STACY LONG: My mother was born and raised here in East Run, and my husband and I chose to build our home here, because it's incredibly peaceful and quiet. There's no traffic lights, no traffic, no storefronts, just homes and fields and farms. Most nights you can see the full Milky Way. When there's a meteor shower we just lie down in the front yard and enjoy the show.

In October 2013, Stacy's mom, Judy Wanchisn, received a public notice from the EPA of a hearing about a frack wastewater injection well being planned for East Run. The well would be situated a half mile from her home, and even closer to the home of her neighbor Jon Perry, who makes his living restoring player pianos. He and his partner live a quarter mile from the proposed waste site and the beautiful Little Mahoning Creek runs through their backyard. As they and many others in the community learned about the evils associated with the practice of frack waste disposal, they became more and more concerned.

Injection Well Threatens Grant Township

Vast deposits of shale gas and oil stretch across America, deep underground. The oil and gas industry is accessing these deposits through a relatively new gas-extracting process, which requires the high-pressure injection of enormous quantities of water and toxic chemicals into the shale formation. "Fracking" has been touted as a method to provide cheaper, cleaner, and more climate-friendly energy to communities. In fact, its effects are harmful, and result in the depletion and poisoning of aquifers, in earthquake activity, and in the release into the air of climate-destructive methane gas as well as other pollutants and cancer-causing chemicals.

After the damage created by construction and drilling, and by the installation of equipment to capture and haul the gas to compressor stations and export terminals, comes the problem of waste disposal. Here is where injection wells enter the picture. An older existing conventional gas well in Grant Township would be converted into storage for oil and gas waste products. It would be classified as a class 2D injection well and need two permits, one from the EPA and one from the Pennsylvania Department of Environmental Protection (DEP). As the chemical components are not required to be disclosed under a congressional exemption known as the "Halliburton Loophole" (after the company that created the loophole), this extremely toxic waste could threaten the health of surrounding communities.

Grant Township has no public water, and residents are responsible for their own wells. Should their water become poisoned, residents would have to buy water. In addition, to be granted any relief for the loss of their water, or for other negative health-related effects, the burden of proof of toxicity would fall on them, and that scientific process inevitably entails great expense. And at that point of course, the damage would already be done.

While researching the problems with injection wells, Judy Wanchisn, Stacy's mom, heard about CELDF through a friend in the League of Women Voters, and contacted Chad Nicholson, who had been working on the ground in Pennsylvania as a CELDF organizer. Nicholson is a young activist with a lot of experience under his belt in post-Katrina New Orleans where the distribution of resources made it clear that corporations would benefit from the disaster. He joined forces with CELDF in 2009, when he moved to Spokane to help in their Bill of Rights campaign.

When Judy Wanchisn asked for his help with a permit appeal, he explained that based on years of CELDF's experience trying to stop the granting of permits, no matter what the experts say about the harms created, the EPA almost always ends up issuing the permit. He was able to point out that other townships stood by helplessly in the face of EPA's approval of these permits. Nicholson continued to explain that therefore CELDF no longer does appeals but that he would be willing to help the community draft an ordinance.

Stacy, her mom, and others willing to do the work; Jon Perry, William Woodcock, Sue Carlson, and Mark Long, decided to form a community group to petition their local government to fight the injection well. They named themselves after an endangered salamander, the Hellbender, an unusually large and colorful species dating back sixty-five million years, and depending for its survival on the water of the Little Mahoning Creek staying pure. The East Run Hellbender Society members talked with neighbors and friends and soon found that nearly every one of their fellow human creatures, whatever their political persuasion, was opposed to the proposed injection well.

The Grant Township elected supervisors meet once a month, so the group went to the April meeting and presented the information they had gathered. Chad Nicholson was invited to speak. He explained the ordinance, and how the current structure of law is set up to benefit corporations like Pennsylvania General Energy (PGE) at the expense of the community's health and safety. But if the community wanted to stand up and assert their rights, the ordinance was the path to follow. The township supervisors including Jon Perry, who had just been asked to fill a seat that had become vacant, decided to proceed with the drafting of an ordinance.

Meetings followed, where the CELDF-generated ordinance was discussed, and where the possible repercussions, in particular, lawsuit from oil and gas corporations, were made clear.

In June 2014, the vote was held, with sixty residents and four lawyers from PGE present in the room. These men threatened the township with a lawsuit if the ordinance was approved. The residents peppered them with questions and instead of backing off, the supervisors had strong support to go ahead and adopt the ordinance. Jon Perry, representing his community, said to the lawyers, "We are not scared of you. Bring it on."

And so it was that the three Grant Township supervisors adopted the first ordinance in the nation that banned the permanent storage of frack wastewater and the deposition of oil and gas waste materials within the community. This Community Bill of Rights Ordinance prohibited the injection well as a violation of the community's rights to clean air and water, and local self-government.

While possessing a similar DNA to the Blaine Township ordinance, the structure of Grant Township's law looks different. CELDF has evolved the rights-based ordinances over the years to invite specific confrontations with the corporations, the state, and the courts. Mainly the ordinances are now designed to force the courts to pick a side and answer the question: Whose rights are greater within the community? The corporation's "rights" or the community's rights?

The evolution of the ordinances are traced through the chapters of this book.

Grant Township Sued by PGE and PIOGA

Just as happened in Blaine, not long after passing their ordinance, in August 2014, Grant Township was sued, in this case in Federal Court by the Pennsylvania General Energy Company, LLC (PGE). In its lawsuit, PGE claimed that it had a "right" to inject wastewater into the township. The Pennsylvania Independent Oil and Gas Association (PIOGA) also filed to intervene in the case, declaring that there is "no constitutional right to local self-government" or to be free from the harms associated with oil and gas production.

The complaint contained thirteen counts, which declared that the township lacked the authority to ban injection wells, and also that the corporations' "rights" were violated. PGE's lawyers contended that the ordinance violated PGE's federal constitutional rights under the First Amendment (free speech), the Fifth Amendment (due process), and the Fourteenth Amendment (equal protection).

As it became clear to Grant Township residents that their community was a sacrifice zone to the gas company, many were enraged. Nicholson said: "When something like this comes down, people have to figure out their priorities, and these supervisors held strong. They decided to move forward and retain CELDF to serve as their legal counsel. The PGE lawyers' strategy was to throw enough stuff to scare the supervisors, lots of depositions and subpoenas, including a motion for injunctive relief, as if they were being grievously harmed by not being able to dump their fracking waste in that one well in Grant Township. The community came together to fight. PGE even put offers on the table to settle, including an offer to withdraw the lawsuit if Grant Township would repeal the ordinance and allow PGE to proceed.

At the same time, the East Run Hellbenders filed to intervene in the lawsuit, represented by Lindsey Schromen-Wawrin, an attorney who collaborates with CELDF. This motion to intervene did so not only on behalf of the Hellbenders, but on behalf of an ecosystem that would be harmed by the injection well, specifically the Little Mahoning Watershed. This was the first time in the U.S. that an ecosystem filed to intervene in court to advocate for its own interests. (See the rights of nature in Chapter 3.)

As all this was occurring, and the community was rallying to provide support and funds to help in the fight, they were also recognizing how few rights they really had under their current status as a township regulated by the state's Second Class Township Code. So Stacy and her mother, started to look into home rule as a way to expand local control over important issues that affect the health and safety of residents.

About Home Rule

Going home rule became an option in Pennsylvania in 1968 when the state constitution was amended to give authority to municipalities to adopt home rule charters, part of a move toward increased local autonomy. Of the approximately 2,500 municipalities in Pennsylvania, around

75 municipalities have achieved this status—the city of Pittsburgh among them—which transfers from state legislature to a locally voter-approved charter greater freedom and control over governing within the community. It's a strenuous yearlong (or longer) process in which at least seven government study commissioners are elected to examine the current form of local government to determine whether it is working for the needs of the community. The commissioners then have the option to write a new charter to remedy inadequacies in the current form of government. This proposed charter is then put to a vote in the municipality.

After Stacy and her mom were elected along with five other study commissioners, they worked hard doing endless paperwork and educating residents. In this process they received guidance from Chad Nicholson, who served as a consultant during the study phase as well as in the drafting of the home rule charter. There were two public hearings. Many township residents do not use email, so they had to hand deliver copies of the charter and educate people that home rule is about pushing back against the energy corporations. They sent a postcard to every voter in Grant Township, asking them to come to the first hearing so they could understand what home rule is. There was some ugliness, yelling, and finger pointing, as a few people feared that Grant Township would not change for the good, but most folks however realized the benefit.

In the summer of 2015 the commissioners' final report criticized the current township system of governance as not adequate to the current needs of the residents. They proposed a charter that would recognize the rights to clean air and water, the right to be taxed fairly, and the right to local community self-government. And it protects those rights by banning frack wastewater injection wells.

For a home rule charter to be adopted, the people of the township must vote it in, and in November 2015, the home rule charter won overwhelmingly by a two to one vote. Interestingly, just a few weeks before the vote, a federal judge invalidated parts of Grant Township's ordinance, stating that the township lacked the authority to ban injections wells. The vote to adopt the charter however reinstated that ban. The people of Grant Township spoke loudly and clearly: they have rights, they will protect those rights, and nobody—not a corporation, not the state government, and not a federal judge—has the authority to tell them that they must accept toxic fracking waste in their community. The transformation of the community into a home rule township invalidated most of that court ruling, as the lawsuit was brought against the ordinance adopted when their status was still a second-class township.

While they were organizing the home rule campaign, Stacy Long put her name on the ballot for supervisor along with her fellow Hellbender, Jon Perry. Both won by a landslide. Neither Jon nor Stacy had ever imagined themselves running for office or serving in municipal government before.

STACY LONG: It's easier to complain. Who wants to write grants, and go to supervisor meetings, but our only hope is to repair ourselves locally. It's a ton of work and it makes me crabby, but I derive strength from my family and my wonderful little community.

The lawsuit is ongoing. To find out how it unfolds, go to the CELDF website for updates.

The residents of the township understand that it's possible the gas company will just decide to go ahead and start bringing in the waste and pay the $300-a-day fine. But just as they were prepared to stand up in the face of a lawsuit, the supervisors do not intend to allow drilling.

JON PERRY: If they are not stopped legally, we will engage in civil disobedience. We will stand in the road in front of those trucks. We hope it doesn't come to that. But other gas companies are watching and we have to be unstoppable.

And so it is that in 2015, Grant Township joined a growing numbers of communities across Pennsylvania and the U.S. that are coming together in a community rights movement, to stand up to a system of law that forces frack waste wells and other harmful practices into communities, and protects corporations over people, communities, and nature.

CHAD NICHOLSON: Communities are saying to the government and corporations, "We're no longer willing to be fracked, poisoned, and polluted." They are mobilizing against a system of law that empowers corporations over communities, and empowers government to preempt communities from protecting their air and water. Communities are saying this is not acceptable, it's not sustainable, it's not democratic, and it's going to change.

Chapter 2
New Hampshire: Reclaiming the Declaration of Independence

Sometimes referred to as "blue gold," water has become an increasingly precious resource on our warming, crowded planet. In many states, water is a subject of heated struggle between those outside the community who want to sell it for profit and residents who want to protect it. The unfortunate truth learned by many communities is that they have little or no control over their own water resources. In order to gain control, they have to be willing to try a new approach.

While some activism in the United States happens independent of historical understanding, many activists look for lessons from the past. One way they can do this is by examining the documents that govern their community, such as a state constitution, or the municipal charter that created their town, city, or county, and then learning how to use those documents to strengthen local control and protect the environment.

Even though many state constitutions have been amended to give corporations more rights than individual communities, they also often contain some stellar sources of law that support the effort to take back our inalienable rights.

The Towns of Nottingham and Barnstead, New Hampshire

Situated in the central southeastern part of New Hampshire, Nottingham and Barnstead are rural communities dating back to the early 1700s. They are about eighteen miles apart, with just under five thousand residents each. Among Nottingham's grantees was Peregrine White, descendant of the first child of English parentage born in New England. According to the United States Census Bureau, water comprises 4 percent of the town's 48.4 square miles. Containing fourteen lakes and ponds, Nottingham is drained by the Pawtuckaway and North rivers, and at one time had seventeen water mills in operation. Not far away, the town of Barnstead in Belknap County is nearly as water rich, lying within the Merrimack River watershed. In summer you can see kids jumping off the town bridge into the river or swinging by a rope from a tree branch far into the middle of the water. With its large grassy commons bordered by white Victorian homes and lush woods, Barnstead recalls an earlier, more idyllic time.

Given the abundance of good water, it's no wonder this part of New Hampshire has been targeted by a handful of water corporations that want to suck a commodity out of the ground that sells at a price higher than that of raw crude oil.

However, these small towns are also places where democracy is still practiced at the local level, in the form of town meetings. In the state of New Hampshire, the annual town meeting is a forum for community decision making in which elected representatives, called selectmen, answer directly to those they represent. Any registered resident may attend a town meeting and vote on every article brought up for discussion. Here decisions, budgetary and otherwise, are made; here officials are elected or selected; here ordinances are passed. Some town meetings can get rowdy, and some even stretch into the following day.

Environmental Assault Threatens Community

In 2001, a company known as USA Springs wanted to put in three wells to withdraw over 430,000 gallons of water a day from the local aquifer for a massive water-bottling operation. These wells were to be situated at the headwaters of Nottingham and nearby Barrington, where most inhabitants rely on wells for their own water supply. USA Springs approached the Nottingham planning board to get the necessary permits. On the first pass, the board, believing that the plant would bring business to Nottingham and add to the tax base, changed the zoning of the property from residential to commercial. As time went on, many Nottingham residents objected, insisting that the plan presented a threat to water quality as well as quantity, and the hearings got volatile. Citizens brought in experts who showed that the operation would drain the bedrock aquifer, pollute the remaining water, and disturb wetlands and wildlife.

Community Group Battles Regulatory System

In response to the actions of USA Springs, an umbrella citizens' group called Save Our Groundwater (SOG) formed in Nottingham and Barrington. Active in SOG was a young woman named Olivia Zink, who was studying for a degree in political science at the University of New Hampshire. She jumped in with both feet to help battle USA Springs.

OLIVIA ZINK: Who owns our water? This company intended to take 430,000 gallons a day to ship overseas to Italy for profit. This really fascinated me, and I wanted to learn more.

So Zink learned how to be an organizer, share information, and work with media, businesspeople, neighbors, and elected officials. "It's all about developing those relationships," she says. SOG hired lawyers and familiarized itself with the state's permitting system. The group met with the governor and state representatives, and learned that there were seven other water-bottling plants going in around the state. In response, SOG helped submit legislation to declare that water is held in the public trust, which was passed by the New Hampshire House of Representatives.

In the meantime, USA Springs went to the New Hampshire Department of Environmental Services, which turned down their permit on twenty-seven counts. A water-draw test showed how in just ten days, even while pumping less water than the proposed operation, the wells in the neighborhood dropped forty feet. USA Springs lawyers said there was nothing to worry about, and that they would fix whatever problems arose. But the startling water-draw test results unified people in the affected communities, and it helped SOG cross political and social boundaries and become strong enough to raise funds to mount a legal case. The test also revealed that the pumping had drawn contaminants deeper into the aquifer. Under the New Hampshire Groundwater Protection Act, these contaminants were considered to have an adverse impact. The Department of Environmental Services denied the permit a second time.

SOG celebrated. USA Springs appealed. One of the reasons for the denial from the Department of Environmental Services was that property adjacent to the site contained buried toxins from a large truck-repair facility. USA Springs bought the additional property and filled in the well with chemicals to decontaminate the area. On the company's third application, the permit was approved. The other twenty-six reasons for the earlier denial were disregarded.

Once the necessary parts of the new permit application were filled in, the community planning board had no real ability to fight back, and the company was given the permit to start pumping. Zink was appalled to realize that USA Springs had received permission to literally steal the community's water.

Local Government Says: "Nothing We Can Do"

After the Department of Environmental Services reversed its decision and issued the new permit, Nottingham elected officials, told the community there was nothing further they could do. A second group, Neighborhood Guardians, then formed to fight the development of USA Springs. Together with SOG, they continued to battle the company through the regulatory system, losing the case on every single permit.

At one point, when USA Springs applied for a new driveway permit, the police chief went to the hearing and spoke on the dangers of having trucks pull out every three minutes and the disastrous effect of fully loaded trucks driving the main thoroughfare between Concord and Plymouth. He was told he had no standing to testify at the hearing. Neither did any other community group. Only USA Springs had standing to testify, and they said it was their right to draw water from their land. After years of appeals, the case ended up squarely in front of the New Hampshire Supreme Court.

Group Turns to CELDF to Help Fight Threat

Zink could see that her activism wasn't accomplishing the results she was looking for. She brought Thomas Linzey to New Hampshire to present the Democracy School to local communities.

OLIVIA ZINK: I saw that we had to start focusing on who was making the decisions. The fight was about water, but it was really deeper than that. It was about who decides what our community looks like.

Barnstead Takes Note

In the meantime, the people in Barnstead had been witnessing what was happening in Nottingham, where so many tax dollars were being spent fighting USA Springs, and in Alton, another community nearby, where a smaller bottling plant was already operational. Barnstead's concerned residents invited SOG to come have a discussion. Zink showed *Thirst*, a documentary about how companies took water from locally built ponds in India and then sold the water back to the very people who had dug the ponds in the first place. Zink compared this example to what was happening in Nottingham, where the regulatory system had failed to help citizens. She asked the people of Barnstead, "Do you really want to spend energy and community resources battling something you won't win, or do you want to try a different way?" To strengthen her case, she talked about how multiple communities in Pennsylvania, with help from CELDF, had recently passed ordinances successfully banning corporations from spreading sludge waste.

This drew the attention of Barnstead resident Gail Darrell because Barnstead had previously passed a resolution against corporate sludge-spreading, but it did not stop the practice. She also knew that people in various other communities were passing resolutions to protect their water but were having no success. Darrell sought more information. A New Hampshire native, homesteader, and gardener, she was a stay-at-home mom, raising her four children and her vegetables in the quiet countryside. She lives in a rustic old home with a welcoming kitchen, where a pot of soup is always simmering on the wood stove. The river runs 150 yards from the house, and the well sits right by the kitchen door, supplying both house and garden. She worried that if the water-bottling plant drained the local aquifer, the area's farmers and their animals would be severely affected.

After attending the Democracy School, Darrell learned that the regulatory system is set up to create a barrier between local residents and corporate entities. This barrier isn't some kind of malfunction; it's built into the system.

GAIL DARRELL: If you have corporations that come into your town, and you do not have a say, you do not live in a democracy. We should start acting like sovereign people who can have an impact and a perspective!

Zink noticed the avid interest from the Barnstead residents.

OLIVIA ZINK: Democracy School is a good tool, but it's using that tool to inform your community that matters. The first school in Barnstead spurred on conversations at the community store, the town hall, and while pumping gas. That first night, people didn't sleep, they pulled out the constitution and returned in the morning, excited and motivated to keep learning.

Group Decides on Rights-Based Course of Organizing

Darrell and other citizens formed a core-group committee with the goal of bringing to the Select Board a real plan for protecting Barnstead's water.

Darrell had lived in the town for many years, and she had a good reputation, so she went door to door, talking to every neighbor, and then traveled further into outlying areas. She talked people into attending public meetings. She told them about the situation in Nottingham and how Barnstead was trying a new approach.

GAIL DARRELL: The most important part of organizing is the day-to-day conversations with neighbors around kitchen tables. That's what builds a strong movement, sharing information and expertise and opinions. The great thing is that people begin to talk, not only about what they are against, but more importantly, what they want their community to look like and what rights they believe they possess.

The Barnstead Select Board met with Thomas Linzey, who asked what the group wanted to do. Selectman Gordon Preston said, "We want you to write us an ordinance," and Selectman Jack O'Neill said, "And we want it to start it with 'We the People.'"

Unified, the governing body of Barnstead agreed they wanted to start their ordinance with a preamble citing that their authority comes from the Declaration of Independence, which declares that governments are instituted to secure people's rights, and that government derives its just powers from the consent of the governed.

Preamble of Barnstead's Ordinance of Rights

Section 2. Preamble and Purpose. We the People of the Town of Barnstead declare that water is essential for life, liberty, and the pursuit of happiness—both for people and for the ecological systems, which give life to all species.

We the People of the Town of Barnstead declare that we have the duty to safeguard the water both on and beneath the Earth's surface, and in the process, safeguard the rights of people within the community of Barnstead, and the rights of the ecosystems of which Barnstead is a part.

We the people of Barnstead declare that all of our water is held in the public trust as a common resource to be used for the benefit of Barnstead residents and of the natural ecosystems of which they are a part.

A community rights gathering in Illinois.

Community Gathers Support for the Ordinance

Among the many people who worked hard to get the ordinance passed were Bruce Shearer and Carolyn Namaste, a couple who have chosen to raise some of their own food and to live close to the land. They strongly believe that they have to practice what they preach when it comes to protecting nature.

BRUCE SHEARER: We're part of the whole living web of life. But the government represents money. I'm not saying there are no good politicians, but really, who's calling the shots? It comes down to who decides here, we the people or we the money.

Selectman Jack O'Neill became one of the ordinance's strongest advocates. Initially, he had supported USA Springs because Barnstead needed the business. But the more he learned about the company's plan, the less he could support it. He decided to personally educate the community, writing letters to the editor, joining in potluck dinners and meetings at the library, publishing articles to keep people informed, and speaking at the American Legion. He helped sway the other four selectmen of the planning board with the argument that if they had an ordinance in place,

USA Springs would not spend a half-million dollars on legal fees, but would instead be motivated to go elsewhere. Thomas Linzey and CELDF had already committed to stand by Barnstead and fight any legal battles that ensued.

An Obstacle: People's Unwillingness to Break Illegal Law

Gail Darrell and other members of her group spent a year of solid organizing, informing community members about the issue and attending every town meeting to remind the Select Board of their duty to do the will of the people. One obstacle she had not planned on encountering was the concern on the part of many about directly challenging the laws that grant corporations constitutional rights. Her group realized that, for some people, going up against established law was a huge and often frightening challenge. Some people got angry with Darrell, reacting negatively to her message. She told them that throughout American history, people have had to challenge settled laws that violate community and human rights. She also assured them that the ordinance did not violate their state constitution.

The Vote in Barnstead

Darrell and Shearer both agree that if neighboring Nottingham hadn't already shown how much time and taxpayer money could be wasted using the regulatory system, the Barnstead ordinance probably would not have passed. When there is a situation close to home that people can identify with, they are more attentive.

So in March 2006, at Barnstead's annual town meeting, the community deemed that the ordinance was the right approach to protect its water, with 135 people voting a resounding "yes" and only one vote against.

Selectman Jack O'Neill, a Vietnam veteran, was proud to pass the ordinance, as was Gordon Preston, who originally moved his family to Barnstead to be near ski country. While wildly different in temperament, both men recognize they have established something that does not simply protect the water in their town, but is groundbreaking law.

GORDON PRESTON: New Hampshire is a good state to pioneer this law in. Because of our structure of town meetings and the wording of our constitution, our judges are extremely reluctant to go after an existing town vote, so it's therefore unlikely it would be overturned.

JACK O'NEILL: I went to war for my country. I have to say, this is the first time in my life I've seen democracy starting to work. We the people of Barnstead threw aside our fears for the generations to come, knowing we were in a battle with the corporations and their legal teams. To the nation, this might be a small battle, but something has to be done, and we the people of the town of Barnstead will walk point.

Regulatory System Fails Nottingham

While the people in Barnstead were being proactive in organizing and passing their ordinance, activist groups in Nottingham had high hopes as their case moved forward to be heard in the New Hampshire Supreme Court. They pinned these hopes on the argument that because groundwater is held in the "public trust," the court should prevent abuse of the groundwater system. They argued that the Department of Environmental Services permit violated the public trust because it allowed privatization of the water supplies.

On July 8, 2007, the New Hampshire Supreme Court issued its decision. It denied that the two community groups had standing in the case and unanimously ruled in favor of the corporation and the state, which had filed a brief supporting the corporation.

Some Nottingham residents had anticipated this possible dead end and started investigating Barnstead's ordinance. Chris and Gail Mills, a long-married couple, attended Democracy School soon after Barnstead passed its ordinance. "I've never gotten involved in doing anything like this before," Chris said, "but I was appalled that USA Springs kept getting permits. I was hoping somebody else would step up, but no one else did, so I said, 'I'll do it myself.'"

In order to educate the town and pass an ordinance similar to the one that had passed in Barnstead, the Mills and others decided to form a group and named it the Nottingham Tea Party. This was before the 2010 rise of the national Tea Party, after which the group renamed themselves the Nottingham Water Alliance. The group was composed of Democrats, Republicans, and Independents. They invited speakers into the community, developed publications, and put together brochures. When they started their work, most of the members of the community considered it too late to do anything about USA Springs. So the Nottingham group created a brochure entitled *It's Not Too Late*. They made the point that an ordinance would protect them in the future if another corporation should come in. And they created displays with a powerful quote generally attributed to Abraham Lincoln:

> I see in the near future a crisis approaching that unnerves me and causes me to tremble for the safety of my country. Corporations have been enthroned and an era of corruption in high places will follow, and the money power of the country will endeavor to prolong its reign by working upon the prejudices of the people until all wealth is aggregated in a few hands and the Republic is destroyed.

John Terninko, who has lived in Nottingham for forty-one years and calls himself a "city kid turned country," came onboard when he signed one of the Mills' petitions. His comments at the Department of Environmental Services hearing reflected his frustration: "I recognize that everything I will say is irrelevant. This company [USA Springs] has violated our trust. They have violated seventeen ordinances in Barrington already, which should be sufficient grounds to not do business with them, but that doesn't stop you at DES from moving forward with the permits. This whole process is a sham."

When the group held meetings, they invited the members of their Select Board to attend, but these representatives, unlike those in Barnstead, declined to participate.

Education and Obstacles

In order to get public support for their ordinance, the Nottingham Water Alliance needed to present their information before a town meeting. Since the Select Board refused to support the ordinance, the group was left to its own resources. They quickly gathered 162 signatures, which they then presented to the town clerk, who had no choice but to place the issue on the upcoming town meeting agenda.

In educating Nottingham residents about the ordinance, the organizers faced several obstacles. The first was the assumption that all business is good business because it brings taxes and jobs. They had to explain that new jobs are often filled from outside town, and that the town's treasury would be severely taxed to pay for the new costs of infrastructure and pollution. A second obstacle was based on an unwillingness to admit that the government wasn't looking out for the public interest. Many people found it hard to give up that hope.

Gail Mills Addressed Another Sticking Point:

GAIL MILLS: Stripping corporations of the rights of persons really confused people. Businesses were getting frightened, calling to say they wouldn't be able to do business in Nottingham any more. We had to explain that it is when corporations use those rights to get their way that they are doing harm, not when they are doing good business.

The fire department chief expressed his concern that the language of the ordinance meant he wouldn't be able to help out other towns with water. The group then created an amendment to the ordinance, identifying the exceptions when organizations such as the fire department, local utilities, the military, and nonprofits would be allowed to use and transport water, as long as they didn't sell the water outside Nottingham.

The ordinance presented by the Nottingham Water Alliance stated that they were relying on Article 10 of New Hampshire's constitution, written in 1784, which says that government is instituted for the whole community and when government fails to provide for the health, safety, or welfare of those they represent, those people have a right to change their system of government.

This Is Called the "Right of Revolution."

In other words, government must serve the needs of the majority, and when other means of redress are ineffectual, people ought to establish a new system of government.

The Nottingham Vote

In March 2008 the town meeting lasted from 8 a.m. to 5 p.m., with 365 people in attendance. The Select Board had the same amount of time to present its position as the Nottingham group, during which they tried to discredit Thomas Linzey and the ordinance. Their stance was that the town had spent a lot of money defending lawsuits and didn't want any more money spent on fighting USA Springs, especially now that the company had obtained all its permits. Regardless of the opinion of the Select Board, the community passed the ordinance with 63 percent of the vote. And to protect it against unilateral action by the Select Board, a clause was written into the ordinance that two-thirds of the community would be needed to overturn it, and this could not happen without a town meeting. Afterward, the Nottingham group sent a registered letter to USA Springs, informing them of the passing of the ordinance and stating that their business plan was in violation of local law.

The right of revolution: Part I, Article 10:

> . . . Government being instituted for the common benefit, protection, and security of the whole community, and not for the private interest or emolument of any one man, family, or class of men; therefore, whenever the ends of government are perverted, and public liberty manifestly endangered, and all other means of redress are ineffectual, the people may, and of right ought to reform the old, or establish a new government. The doctrine of nonresistance against arbitrary power, and oppression, is absurd, slavish, and destructive of the good and happiness of mankind. . . .

USA Springs stopped building when the ordinance passed, and soon after filed for bankruptcy. Group members kept up pressure on the Select Board by reminding them of their duty to enforce the ordinance. They were also not afraid to remind members of the Select Board of Article 8 of the New Hampshire Constitution, which states that it is the duty of elected officials to execute the will of the people, and if they don't, they may be removed.

OLIVIA ZINK: Now I can share with other people that this is what the residents of New Hampshire are doing to take back their water supply. It may seem strange to say, but I hope the ordinance gets challenged because it will present an opportunity, a tool to spread the message wider.

GAIL DARRELL: People say: "You passed the ordinance in Barnstead? How did you do that?" I tell them you have to be willing to take the time to talk to people, lots of people, about what you see as the problem. It takes perseverance, a person who's committed and who doesn't give up. To be effective, you have to learn from what you do and keep going, and you have to keep the faith and the hope, because these fights are long and there are many losses along the way. But how else am I going to answer to my children?

UPDATE: The Barnstead and Nottingham Ordinances Stand

Ten years after the communities of Barnstead and Nottingham passed their ordinances, those laws still stand. And ten other communities have adopted rights-based ordinances protecting community health, safety, and welfare, by prohibiting harmful activities that would violate the rights of the community. Along with commercial water extraction and gravel mining, activities now covered under rights-based ordinances include unsustainable energy systems like industrial wind and large-scale hydroelectric projects. Those ordinances enshrine the right to access pure water, clean air, the peaceful enjoyment of home, scenic preservation, and local community self-government.

In order to make sure their particular ordinance was enforced, the folks in Nottingham continued to battle the USA Springs bottling plant for eight years until finally, in 2014, the corporation's permit expired. The group held a celebration party, at which they burned the permit in a fire pit.

After USA Springs went into bankruptcy, the company spent years looking for investors. They needed some $60 million to climb out of debt and continue with plans for the new plant. Chris and Gail Mills went to every single bankruptcy hearing. When they learned of a new potential investor, they would make sure that the investor received a copy of Nottingham's ordinance. This happened seven times, with investors from not only the U.S. but also Europe, and every time, being aware of the ordinance's content quickly put an end to interest. Eventually USA Springs tried to stop the names of potential investors being revealed to the public. That effort failed and after eight years, the state did not renew the permits. The Nottingham Water Alliance's hard work and vigilance paid off.

GAIL MILLS: We showed that a handful of people can fight off an international company. You need a few committed people and you have to show people you are serious. It may take a long time, but it's not too late.

Sugar Hill and the Northern Pass

In the meantime, the Hydro-Quebec corporation proposed a power project called the Northern Pass that would use the state's lands for high-tension transmission lines to carry electrical power to the Southern Tier (MA and CT), with no access for, or benefit to, New Hampshire people.

It would begin in the northern part of state and traverse much of New Hampshire to connect to existing power lines in the south of lakes region. Such a 180-mile route of high voltage transmission wires and steel towers reaching 140 feet in height would create a permanent scar on some of the state's most pristine rural locations.

Of the many communities that would be deleteriously affected, Easton and Sugar Hill were the first two municipalities to adopt via town meeting, Right to a Sustainable Energy Future and Local Self-Governance Bill of Rights Ordinances by overwhelming margins in 2012, to prohibit corporate energy infrastructure from being built within the town. These ordinances ban the building of unsustainable energy projects while codifying into law the communities' right to a sustainable energy future, their right to local self-governance, and elevating communities' rights over corporate rights.

The town of Plymouth enacted a similar ordinance a few days later. This town has already moved forward with creating a Sustainable Energy Policy. The first part of the local plan, already in place, is a solar-generated system with a capacity of 60 MW that operates the municipal water and sewer system.

Over the next years, to the west of these towns, Grafton became the fourth community to adopt a Community Bill of Rights in 2013 against unsustainable energy systems. This was in response to the many proposed industrial wind tower projects for the Newfound Lake and Mount Cardigan region. Such projects would negatively impact both the scenic tourist attraction of the mountaintop communities and the sensitive ecosystems of watersheds and wildlife, with local residents reaping all of the disruption and costs and little of the rewards of such a commercial project. In 2014 Alexandria, Danbury, and Hebron joined the other four towns in Grafton County to enact similar Community Bills of Rights (CBOR). Their ordinances prohibit industrial wind projects from siting in the town.

All of the Right to a Sustainable Energy Future Ordinances contain a provision for the town to create its own Sustainable Energy Policy thus prompting conversation and planning on how to generate their own energy. As Plymouth demonstrated with its solar-generated system, municipalities have much to gain by implementing their own local renewable systems, thereby becoming more energy secure.

New Hampshire Community Rights Network

Fighting off different kinds of unwanted projects made it abundantly clear to the organizers on the ground that they were caught in a repetitive loop, going through the same process Barnstead and Nottingham had gone through with water rights, over and over and over. So in April 2013, folks from communities that had been active and from communities such as Swanzey and Jaffrey that were interested in becoming active, came together to form the New Hampshire Community Rights Network (NHCRN). Through conference calls and quarterly meetings members find support and share skills and insight. They are holding workshops to broaden their educational efforts across the state. They especially want to reach out to the southern, more urban communities that are threatened by a Kinder Morgan pipeline.

Michelle Sanborn, a stay-at-home mom who honed her organizing skills getting the Community Bill of Rights for Sustainable Energy passed in Alexandria, Grafton County, is the coordinator of the NHCRN. Fighting off corporate wind projects threatening her beloved mountainscape, she had recognized that the power to make decisions rested not with those affected by the development but with a state agency. She also experienced a steep learning curve coming up against the attitude that development is a "good" not to be questioned. Together with other committed residents, she managed to educate her community and pass the ordinance in spite of their selectmen. Barnstead's Gail Darrell mentored them in their endeavor. Since Darrell's sad and untimely death in 2015, Sanborn has also become the chair of NHCRN's governing board.

As the New Hampshire Community Rights Network met, it became obvious that in order not to have to mount each campaign and fight in each community separately, and in order to validate the various ordinances permanently, what was needed was a constitutional amendment to New Hampshire's constitution. So they produced and signed an inspirational founding document called the Barnstead Declaration. (See Appendix.) Based on the calls for constitutional change that are part of each Community Bill of Rights ordinance that has been enacted in the state of New Hampshire, the declaration proposes to amend the Constitution of the State of New Hampshire.

MICHELLE SANBORN: When it comes to our government, no one wants to look at alternatives. But who best to protect the environment but

Chapter 3
Tamaqua and Pittsburgh: Recognizing Nature's Right to Exist

IN NATURE, ONE CREATURE'S WASTE IS often recycled as another's food. Increasingly, human waste has become a toxic mix of the by-products of commercial and industrial production. This has had serious consequences for the environment. Many of us still hold to the notion that we can "throw things away" without realizing that a place "away" from everything else never did exist. More often than not, throwing something away these days means dumping it in someone else's community—usually a poor community, either urban or rural, where people don't have the clout to fight these practices.

Tamaqua Borough in Pennsylvania is one such place. After years of absorbing egregious amounts of toxic waste, Tamaqua grew tired of trying to get environmental protection laws to work for them. A sick environment will create sick people, so it's no coincidence that a local nurse banded together with a patient and a doctor to try a new way of getting governmental action.

They recognized that they would never find protection under the current structure of law, which treats natural communities and ecosystems as property, intended for human use, profit, and exploitation. "Ecosystems" are defined as all of the flora, fauna, and features and systems of the natural environment that support that life; "natural communities" are a subset of ecosystems—dealing just with flora and fauna.

Because they had come to recognize that their lives were not separate from nature, but instead profoundly interdependent, the people in Tamaqua sought to have their local laws reflect this new understanding. This meant they would have to discard the old notion of "environmental protection" and instead learn to think of ecosystems as having their own inalienable rights.

The borough councilmembers and the mayor of Tamaqua struggled to come to agreement about this innovative law. As in many other communities, some representatives were determined to try something new on behalf of their constituents, while others balked at the possibility of being sued by companies whose activities might be banned or challenged by state officials beholden to such companies. The people of Tamaqua had to realize that as long as they were operating in fear of such an eventuality, they were not free to decide what was best for their own community. They decided to cast off that fear.

Sludge Dumping Threatens Tamaqua

Tamaqua is a borough of about seven thousand people located one hundred miles west of Philadelphia, in eastern Schuylkill County, Pennsylvania. According to its residents, Tamaqua is a Native American name for "running water," although others say it means "land of the beaver." On certain days, the rivers that run through town turn an oily yellow-orange from the toxic runoff of old coal mines. No beavers have been sighted near these waters for years.

Tamaqua is situated within the Pennsylvania coal region of the Appalachian Mountains. Coal mining was an extremely vital economic activity in the region throughout the twentieth century, but it has since experienced a decline. What remain are gigantic pits, in some cases twice the size of nearby towns.

Early in the twenty-first century, pit owners started being able to turn a profit by inviting companies outside the state to use their sites as dumping grounds for industrial and wastewater sludge. Euphemistically called "biosolids," sludge contains a number of toxic substances, which leach into local aquifers, rivers, and reservoirs.

In Tamaqua, there are no protections offered against leaching. The runoff goes into the rivers and creeks that run by the homes of Tamaqua to join the Little Schuylkill River, which feeds the larger Schuylkill, which then goes on to supply the city of Philadelphia. In 2004, during a series of hearings with the Department of Environmental Protection, residents were given the opportunity to ask questions about the process of sludge dumping. During one of these sessions, they discovered that the Lehigh Coal and Navigation Company planned to start filling old mine pits not only with sludge, but also with fly ash—a fine, powdery substance generated in the combustion of coal. This process would turn Tamaqua's old mine pits into unlined landfills for toxic waste and coat the town with poisonous dust.

Department of Environmental Protection officials made public statements to the effect that biosolids and fly ash are not harmful to the environment, and that Tamaqua should feel grateful for the local income, as Lehigh Coal was offering the borough a dollar for every ton of fly ash dumped. The residents of Tamaqua and surrounding boroughs were not easily persuaded. They had already put up with years of government indifference to the rising incidence of disease in their township associated with environmental pollution.

Tamaqua Targeted in the Past

Cathy Miorelli is a registered nurse who works at the local public high school. She and her husband were both born in Tamaqua. She knows all too well that her community is a hotbed of toxic exposure. Within miles of Tamaqua are three toxic Superfund sites operated by three corporations: McAdoo Associates, the Tonolli Corporation, and Eastern Diversified Metals. The area is also home to a number of industrial facilities, including a handful of waste-coal-burning power plants.

Over the years, Miorelli became increasingly aware of the number of recurring illnesses among students at the high school, as well as the high incidence of various cancers, thyroid problems, and multiple sclerosis in the community. Stonewalled by the state's Department of Health and the Department of Environmental Protection, she decided to run for the local council. After she was elected, she explained her foray into politics:

CATHY MIORELLI: I have always been concerned about those that don't have a voice. I got involved for fear of my own children and their safety, wanting the air and water to be safe for them and all the children in school. I ran for office because I wasn't happy with what was being done, or not being done, and too many officials just wanted to take care of their friends.

Through Dr. Peter Baddick, who practices internal medicine in nearby Carbon County, Miorelli met longtime county resident Joe Murphy, who was diagnosed with multiple sclerosis a few years ago. Murphy's family has lived in the borough for five generations. He is articulate and well-informed. After being diagnosed, he did some research and discovered that

Cathy Miorelli and Joe Murphy of Tamaqua Borough.

Tamaqua has a much higher rate of multiple sclerosis and cancer than the national average. Why, he wondered, was Tamaqua experiencing such elevated illness levels?

Murphy eventually found out that, along with its well-known Superfund sites, the area has long been a notorious site for illegal "midnight dumpers" unloading toxic waste. Among the volatile byproducts in the soil are arsenic, lead, cadmium, zinc, chromium, manganese, trichloroethylene, mercury, PCBs, and vinyl chloride. These chemicals were being mixed with other chemicals, such as lye, and covered up with a coating of earth and grass.

Murphy and Baddick had spent years talking to the Department of Health and the Department of Environmental Protection, alerting them to the high incidence of cancer and other diseases in the borough. They were told there was no way the area could have been contaminated.

When they finally got through to an epidemiologist, they were told their analysis had been correct all along, and that the government agencies were not correctly analyzing their own statistics.

Murphy took a jaded look at the experience: "There's no brass ring to come out and investigate—only to facilitate the bureaucracy. People think these departments are doing their job of protecting us, but it's not the case."

Miorelli and Murphy came together, thinking that if they could demonstrate that the local cancer cluster was linked to toxic contamination, perhaps they could at least stop the current dumping. They instead found members of the town planning board happy to take the word of various state agencies and corporate officials. For a short time, Lehigh Coal had been forced to stop dumping due to permit violations and non-payment of back taxes, but the Department of Environmental Protection decided to pay for the company's tax bill and then grant it a new permit. Miorelli could see the corruption happening right in front of her. It was clear that conventional methods were not going to help.

Contact with CELDF

As part of her councilmember activities, Miorelli attended a meeting in another town where an activist named Ben Price spoke. Price worked in the corporate world as a manager in a trucking company before taking on full-time work as a Democracy School teacher and member of CELDF.

BEN PRICE: The work is endless and the days off are few, but I'm happier doing this than [my other] job. It has transformed my outlook on life. And the best thing is when I meet someone like Cathy Miorelli, someone willing to take a stand.

Through Price, Cathy Miorelli met Antoinette and Russell Pennock, whose son Daniel died after being exposed to toxic sludge, which had been dumped on the farmland next door to their home. For Miorelli, the couple's grief made the stakes crystal clear. Impressed with Price's broad knowledge about sludge dumping in Pennsylvania communities, as well as his dedication to providing alternative strategies for fighting the practice, Miorelli decided to attend Democracy School.

Democracy School

The Democracy School was held in an adjacent township, and was attended by supervisors from many communities that were struggling with sludge dumping. Miorelli was the only person at the school from Tamaqua. She was completely energized by the experience. Afterward, she was motivated to encourage Tamaqua to be in the forefront of the fight against sludge dumping.

CATHY MIORELLI: After the Democracy School, I was permanently changed. Most importantly, I learned that we have rights as a local government. I realized that we could act on what we wanted most and put together an ordinance that would prevent contaminants from coming into our town.

Miorelli also learned, however, that all existing environmental laws in the United States are anchored in the concept of nature as property, and were passed under the authority of the U.S. Constitution's Commerce Clause. She was reminded that not so long ago in our country, people were property too. Thomas Linzey explains:

> Until slavery was abolished, a slave master could not be punished for whipping a slave, because that slave was his property, and he had the right to damage it. Until the 1900s in some states rape was "property damage," because women lacked the rights of persons. The suffragists and the abolitionists were running up against a structure of law that would not allow them to make the changes they needed. Under our constitution, you're either a person or you are property. What movements do is move and transform that. We won't have a real environmental movement in this country until we realize that nature has rights.

For Miorelli, providing rights to nature seemed self-evident. As she started sharing her new views, her excitement encouraged a few of her colleagues and fellow activists to hold a Democracy School in Tamaqua. With help from CELDF, in 2006, the group drafted an ordinance banning the dumping of sludge. In Tamaqua, an ordinance must first be proposed and advertised before it can be voted on by the town council. Leading this effort alongside Miorelli was the mayor of Tamaqua Borough, Chris Morrison, who realized in his meetings with state legislators that the sludge industry's billion-dollar profits and lobby carried more weight than the health concerns of a small group of people.

CHRIS MORRISON: Tamaqua is where I am going to stay and create my future. Our biggest issue is taking care of the environment, and I have brought it to the forefront in my tenure as mayor.

The citizens of Tamaqua wanted their local laws to recognize that natural communities and ecosystems possess a fundamental right to exist and flourish, and that residents of those communities possess the legal authority to enforce those rights on behalf of the ecosystem.

As Morrison, Miorelli, and others distributed information leaflets door to door, they were able to make personal contact with people; this was a hugely important organizing tool to garner the necessary support. Local newspapers also gave the ordinance some positive coverage, which is not usually the case.

Tamaqua Ordinance

An ordinance was created to protect the health, safety, and general welfare of the people and environment of Tamaqua Borough by banning corporations from engaging in the land application of sewage sludge, by banning persons from using corporations to engage in land application of sewage sludge, by providing for the testing of sewage sludge prior to land application in the borough, by removing constitutional powers of corporations within the borough, and by recognizing and enforcing the rights of residents to defend natural communities and ecosystems.

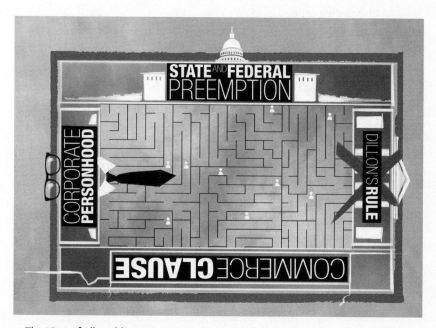

The "Box of Allowable Activism": Communities find themselves in the middle of the box, facing off against corporate legal doctrines which override the people's right of local, community self-government.

Obstacles

As Miorelli and others worked to organize support, one constant obstacle they encountered was that people were too busy to get educated. It was much easier for them to believe that the government would keep them safe rather than finding out for themselves what these pollutants had the potential to do. Unfortunately, it's only when people are directly threatened that they seem to get motivated, so the task of organizers was to make the dangers to the community more tangible.

The rights for nature spelled out in the ordinance also proved a contentious issue. Opponents felt that rights should not be given to something that isn't "alive and/or not a person." Proponents affirmed that, just as children don't have full legal rights but still deserve to be protected, so, too, should nature be protected. They also pointed out that the ordinance would not stop the free use of private property except where such use interfered with the existence and vitality of the overall ecosystem.

Eliminating the authority of a property owner to completely destroy the ecosystem would be far more effective than trying to regulate how much harm an ecosystem could sustain.

Miorelli also faced an uphill battle with her fellow councilmembers. A few of them liked the dollar-a-ton deal offered by Lehigh Coal, and they believed the statements released by the Department of Energy stating that the dumping was safe. Some councilmembers also had personal associations with various coal companies.

But perhaps the most daunting obstacle to the township passing a challenging form of legislation was the threat of being sued. The Tamaqua solicitor, who saw the purpose of his job as keeping the town council safe from potential lawsuits, spoke strongly against passing the ordinance. He warned that it could be interpreted as challenging state law. Such warnings often end up giving corporations even more power, as the threat of a lawsuit discourages many from enacting measures to curtail corporate activity. It isn't only the township that can be sued, but also potentially the individual members of the town council. Each member of the council has to face down this threat in their own way.

Mayor Chris Morrison's response was clear: "If I am going to be sued, so be it. You want to take my row home, my little car, good luck, you can have them. We are going to protect our community."

Miorelli knew that the Tamaqua council vote would probably be split, so she managed to get a large crowd to attend the council meeting in order to put pressure on the representatives. At the meeting, she read aloud a portion of the Pennsylvania State Constitution that specifically acknowledges local control.

The mayor cast the deciding vote, and the borough of Tamaqua passed the anti-sludge ordinance, becoming, in late 2006, the first community in the United States to recognize ecosystems and nature as having rights.

Tamaqua Passes a Second Ordinance

Following the success of the ordinance, the borough council passed a second ordinance the following spring banning anything else the waste corporations might want to haul in. At one of the many public meetings, a representative from the Department of Environmental Protection came to defend the dumping permits. She declared there was no evidence of fly ash being unsafe. Before a crowded room of over a hundred citizens, the mayor confronted her.

CHRIS MORRISON: I asked her if she would like to put a teaspoon of fly ash in her water glass and mix it up and drink it. She said, "Absolutely not." I then said, "You won't drink it, but it's okay for us to breathe it?"

Tamaqua Ordinance

Section 6.6: It shall be unlawful for any corporation or its directors, officers, owners, or managers to interfere with the existence and flourishing of natural communities or ecosystems, or to cause damage to those natural communities and ecosystems.

Enforcement

Despite the new ordinances, coal companies still intended to fill up the community's mine pits with fly ash. When the council received a letter from the Department of Environmental Protection telling them that permits had indeed been granted to dump fly ash in the borough, the council responded with a letter containing their ordinance and stating that they would enforce it.

The Tamaqua ordinances state that if the borough doesn't enforce the sludge ban, individuals in the community are authorized to do so themselves. Should the case arise that local enforcement officers are negligent in enforcing the ordinances, Miorelli and others are ready to do so. CELDF has promised free legal assistance if and when the time comes for them to act.

Packer Township

A few months after the ordinance passed in Tamaqua, Cathy Miorelli learned that thirty-three dump-truck loads of New Jersey sewage sludge had been dumped on a field about seventy-five yards from the Still Creek Reservoir, which lies in Packer Township, Carbon County, and provides drinking water for Tamaqua and other communities. At first, the Department of Environmental Protection claimed there was no record of sludge being dumped, and that they couldn't find any permits. But like all good activists, Miorelli was nothing if not persistent. In response to more pressure, a representative from the Department of Environmental Protection said it was "lime" that had been dumped by the reservoir, not sludge. He then corrected himself after Miorelli sent him photos of the dump site. She also succeeded in getting local media to print stories, letters, and an editorial that put a spotlight on Packer Township. Then she talked to Tom Gerhart, Chair of the Packer Township Board of Supervisors, and told him about the Tamaqua ordinance.

In 2008, the Packer Township supervisors unanimously passed an ordinance to ban sludge dumping, along with stripping corporate rights and giving ecosystems rights instead. Officials from the attorney general's office asked to meet privately with the township supervisors, who proceeded to resist the state's attempt to talk them into dropping the ordinance.

The attorney general filed a lawsuit against the township, using public money to claim that the state had not given Packer Township authority to make a law regarding the use of waste. This action was facilitated by the recently passed so-called "ACRE" (Agricultural Communities and Rural Environments) law, which authorizes the Pennsylvania attorney general to file a lawsuit against any municipality that passes ordinances limiting or restricting "normal agricultural operations." In effect this means the state's top law-enforcement officer can act as private litigator for various corporate agricultural industries, in this case the waste-hauling industries that service the agricultural sector.

CELDF volunteered to represent the township at no cost. At first the members of the board of supervisors stood by their ordinance, refusing to rescind, and refusing to negotiate away any portion of it. It was clear to them that the ACRE law was not passed to aid family farmers, but to buttress agribusiness interests using the legislature as a vehicle and was inherently undemocratic in its nature.

As the Packer Township lawsuit extended over a number of years, however, Tom Gerhart left the supervisors and was elected county commissioner. CELDF offered to help the community transition toward home rule, as the ACRE law does not apply to home rule communities. But subsequent changes in their board, as had happened in Blaine, made the supervisors and community hesitant to go forward with the work and less ready to fight the lawsuit, so they rescinded the ordinance after it became clear that the sludge dumping had voluntarily ceased. To this day, no sludge has been dumped in Packer Township.

CELDF Reframes and Adapts Ordinances

In regards to lawsuits, one strategic goal, though not the final goal, is to get the court to start looking at the constitutional issues involved in the systemic violation of community rights. But lower court judges won't consider constitutional issues if they can find a different non-constitutional reason for overturning the law. So for example, if a law can be struck on the basis of its conflict with a state law, then a lower court is less likely to explore the constitutional issues raised by a local law that challenges state law for violating rights. Most of the time communities that have passed ordinances don't get their day in court to argue that their rights are a distinct issue, that their rights as citizens to clean air and water are above and beyond the authority of the state to make preemptive and regulatory law that deprive people of those rights.

Because of this, CELDF started changing the ordinances and charter amendments they drafted, framing them to force courts to deal with constitutional issues. In the Grant Township fight (see Chapter 1) both the corporations and court have begun to look at and comment on community rights, but not to the degree that would address the residents concerns. CELDF began by reframing ordinances to address systemic rights violations, beginning with Licking Township and then the city of Pittsburgh.

Each iteration of these local laws made it clearer that the intent of the ordinances was to correct illegitimate violation of the right to self-government and that these rights are independently enforceable against both corporations and government entities.

Battling Fracking in Pennsylvania

In October 2010, tiny Licking Township, population five hundred, blazed a big trail in becoming the first municipality to pass an ordinance banning corporations from dumping frack wastewater within its borders. Earlier, in 2002, this same township was the first community in the U.S. to enact a local law stripping corporations of personhood rights.

The Marcellus formation is an organic rich black shale deposited about 390 million years ago, source rock for many conventional oil and gas reservoirs in the Appalachian basin, which is prevalent through most of Pennsylvania at different depth and thickness. Fracking has been demonstrated to be a threat to surface and groundwater and has been blamed for fatal explosions and the contamination of drinking water, rivers, and streams. Because it disturbs rock that's laced not only with methane but with carcinogens like benzene and radioactive ores like uranium, forcing the mix to the surface adds to the dangers.

Prohibiting the introduction of frack wastewater into the township's environment, Licking's new law effectively blocked hydro-fracturing. In addition to banning corporate disposal of frack wastewater, Licking Township's ordinance asserted the right to local self-government and the community's right to a healthy environment and to clean water. In adopting the ordinance, Licking Township legally recognized that nature has rights and doubled down on its eight-year-old subordination of corporate constitutional rights to the rights of human and natural communities.

By recognizing the rights of nature, Licking boldly protected ecosystems and natural communities within the township from efforts by corporations to drill there—or by higher levels of governments to authorize that drilling. Residents of the community became empowered by the language of the ordinance to enforce those rights on behalf of threatened ecosystems.

Pittsburgh Makes History with Their Ordinance

One month later, in November 2010, the City Council of Pittsburgh unanimously adopted a first-in-the-nation ordinance banning corporations from natural gas drilling in the city. It was a Community Bill of Rights that also embraced the rights of nature as legally enforceable. How did this milestone happen?

Corporations had already purchased leases to drill in the city, so in early 2010, in response to the threat, a small group of concerned residents formed Marcellus Protest, a grassroots organization. Pittsburgh's residents did not trust that the corporations would voluntarily protect the community, nor that the legislature or the Pennsylvania Department of Environmental Protection would step up. They had seen that in spite of growing community opposition, the state continued to issue permits to mining corporations to drill. They knew that elected officials and government agencies had long worked with corporations to exempt natural gas drilling and fracking from federal regulations and passed state laws preempting municipalities from taking steps to rein in the industry. They also knew that even communities with zoning restrictions requiring drilling pads to be located away from homes or schools found that its adverse effects still reached into the places they needed to protect.

Members of Marcellus Protest were working to educate residents about fracking and staging protests against the oil and gas industry in Pennsylvania when CELDF organizer Ben Price met online with city councilmember Bill Peduto, along with representatives of over twenty other environmental groups and land use legal eagles. Peduto was looking for a better approach to protecting the city and was openly skeptical of regulatory and zoning "solutions." Hearing about the ordinance recommended by CELDF, he embraced the possibility to not work on minimizing harm but actually stop the harm from happening. He passed on a draft of the ordinance to his colleague Councilman Doug Shields. Ben Price then met Shields at a neighborhood meeting where folks were expressing their fears and concerns. Taking seriously his responsibility to represent the residents of his district and keep them from harm, he decided to sponsor the bill.

The Pittsburgh law contains provisions that eliminate corporate "personhood" rights within the city for corporations seeking to drill, and removes the ability of corporations to wield the Commerce and Contracts

Clauses of the U.S. Constitution to override community decision making. The ordinance elevates the rights of people, the community, and nature over corporate "rights" and challenges the authority of the state to preempt community decision making. This is groundbreaking law, and Pittsburgh thus became the first city in the nation to reignite the debate over who has rights and who will govern.

In June 2010, of the nine councilmembers, there were two in favor, four doubters, and a few opposed. Councilman Shields held a number of hearings and invited industry people and legal experts to testify. He spent many hours explaining and advocating for the ordinance and persuading his fellow councilmembers who were also under great pressure from their own constituents.

The people of Pittsburgh, many of whom aligned themselves with the ad hoc group known as Marcellus Protest, came out in numbers to put pressure on each of the nine councilmembers. Leading up to the time of enactment they held a march with at least eight hundred people carrying banners, pausing to speechify, chant and sing through the city. Some banners proudly proclaimed the constitutional right to clean air and water.

Among the original opponents of the Pittsburgh Community Bill of Rights on city council there had been some ridiculing discussion of the idea of codifying the "Rights of Nature" in city law. But for supporters this was one of the inspirational points of the ordinance. It brought out new allies, such as the Thomas Merton Center and the Unitarian Church as well as some of the more ethically motivated environmentalists.

The industry and their lawyers threatened an immediate lawsuit against the city if the bill passed, but the councilmembers responded that their oath of office required them to represent their constituents' right to a safe environment. In the months leading up to the fateful vote, the ordinance's sponsor, Councilman Shields was a passionate spokesperson for the ordinance.

Councilman Doug Shields: The city is not a colony of the state and will not sit quietly by as our city gets drilled. This fight is about far more than drilling; it's about our authority as a community to decide, not corporations deciding for us. With this vote we are asserting the right of the city to make critical decisions to protect our health, safety, and welfare.

Clearly many others agreed with the councilman, as he was joined by five cosponsors, and all nine councilmembers voted to pass the ordi-

Pittsburgh City Councilman Doug Shields.

nance. This made Pittsburgh the first major U.S. municipality to recognize legally binding rights of nature. By recognizing the rights of nature, Pittsburgh is effectively protecting ecosystems and natural communities within the city from efforts by corporations to drill there—and by other levels of government to authorize that drilling. Residents of Pittsburgh are empowered by the ordinance to enforce those rights on behalf of threatened ecosystems.

Chapter 4
Spokane, Washington: A Bill of Rights for Neighborhoods, Labor, and the Spokane River

IN SMALLER COMMUNITIES, ORGANIZING OFTEN BEGINS in reaction to a specific threat; in a large community, residents usually have a host of concerns that need to be addressed in order to create a vision for the city as a whole. One possible and very effective way to translate this vision into reality is to mount a campaign to add a bill of rights to the city charter. Forty-three states currently have home rule statutes or constitutional provisions that allow for a city to adopt a new charter, or to amend a charter already in existence. A city or county charter is akin to a local constitution.

The ensuing citywide conversation will involve various groups coming together to decide the rights to adopt, and then to define the language that best expresses those rights. This process can be both painstaking and exciting, and it starts with good community organizers who know how to get the conversation going. Democracy in action can get rowdy and contentious, and it demands of us commitment and a deep faith in ourselves and in each other.

Spokane and Its Residents' Concerns
Spokane is the metropolitan center of the Inland Northwest, located on the Spokane River in eastern Washington. It's a classic American city with about two hundred thousand people living in the city proper and about half a million counting the surrounding county. The natural world is visibly in abundance here and has long attracted outdoor sports enthusiasts and tourists. Spokane's Expo '74 is recognized as the world's first environmental fair.

The Spokane metropolitan area has seen an influx of new residents in recent years, and the downtown area has undergone a major rebirth, attracting the development of over five hundred projects worth over $2 billion. The Spokane River runs through downtown in a series of mighty falls that give the town its characteristic beauty. Once a major area for salmon fishing and a natural gathering place for dozens of Northwest native tribes, the river is now one of the most polluted in the country and the salmon have completely disappeared due to construction of dams.

The city of Spokane covers an area of 68.7 square miles. Its population is largely white. About 20 percent of the population lives below the poverty line. Virtually every social class is represented in Spokane's twenty-seven neighborhoods, many of which are of such charm and character that they are recognized on the National Register of Historic Places. Each neighborhood has its own citizen council that meets regularly to discuss pressing issues. An assembly of these councils makes recommendations to the city government. Two of the pressing issues for many neighborhoods are adequate housing and overdevelopment.

Neighborhoods and Development

In Spokane, as in a number of other places, developers and neighborhood communities are often at odds about specific projects proposed. For example, one developer wanted to build a high-rise condominium on a hill overlooking a quaint, relatively low-income neighborhood called Peaceful Valley. The people in the neighborhood objected, as the building would tower over their homes and block out light, clog limited road access, and destroy the old-growth pines on the hillside below where the development was planned. Against all objections, the city government went ahead and approved a building permit for the condo development.

Lori Aluna, Sally Combelic, and Patty Norton—members of the Peaceful Valley neighborhood council—voiced their frustration in running up against the structure of power. The reality is that the councils have no real power because members of the city government do not have to follow any of their advisory suggestions.

LORI ALUNA: We need a different way of governing that isn't the people with power and money influencing the other people with power and money and controlling everyone else.

These women have demonstrated a rare persistence, in part due to a driving sense of justice. They are outraged that the developers say things like, "Well, just sell your house if you don't like what we're doing." These women do not consider their houses as assets but as homes. Indeed, they share a deep love for and commitment to their little neighborhood. They won a small victory when the city appeals process sided with them. But when the developer threatened the city with a lawsuit, the ruling was overturned. They are dreading the day construction starts. Aluna voices the thoughts of many residents:

LORI ALUNA: Why are the trees on the slope considered expendable? Until we stop seeing the planet as a resource that is ours to consume instead of the place that supports our life, we're heading toward our own extinction. Why can't we make a little less money, build affordable housing, and leave the trees?

In another area of town, residents of the Southgate neighborhood objected when a corporation put in an application to build three big-box stores. The residents opposed the plan—claiming it would destroy the area's natural environment and create a huge infrastructure problem for the neighborhood—and appealed to the city council. They brought in planning and environmental experts to speak on their behalf.

Brad Read, a popular high-school teacher as well as a longtime activist, served on the Spokane City Human Rights Commission for five years. He went to the big-box hearing in the city council chambers and said that what he saw felt like the movie *Groundhog Day*. The neighborhood presented its case in front of the hearing examiner and the experts testified. When they finished, the city planner and the representative of the development corporation got up and informed the hearing examiner that, by law, he was bound to ignore virtually all of the testimony presented by the neighborhood group because the only person who had legal standing was the woman who lived next door to one of the parcels of land in question. Then the appeal permit was granted. The neighborhood residents were clearly not the constituency being served under this law.

BRAD READ: The neighbors had done the hard work of local democracy by gathering to defend their community against an unwanted assault, and they were told by the structure of law and governance that their views and concerns didn't matter.

In both of the above situations, while the law governing development recognized the rights of the development corporation, it did not recognize that the neighborhood had any rights to reject the development.

These communities learned that the law endows corporations with constitutional "rights" that are automatically violated when a neighborhood attempts to stop a project. Thus neighborhoods are almost always on the losing end of any decision. While the city of Spokane has a process in place for exercising local control, in reality, residents lack the ability to exercise such control.

Brad Read and Kai Huschke in Spokane.

Work and Unions

Separately, the big-box stores raised other issues of concern. Along with chain stores and fast-food restaurants, big-box stores often drive smaller, locally owned businesses out of business, creating economic dislocation and despair. The jobs they offer tend to be low-wage and without benefits. Company owners use many tactics, such as the threat of job loss, to stall and oppose labor organizing. Unions in Spokane have long been working toward unionization for employees of the big-box stores, but without much success. Constitutional rights such as the right to privacy, free speech, and assembly, as well as due process, have never existed in the private workplace, at least not for workers. The lack of these constitutional protections makes it difficult for members of labor unions to take action to improve wages and the work environment.

The Spokane River

The state of the Spokane River is of huge concern to many in the region. A number of manufacturing companies have located in the area, drawn by the easy access to raw materials and cheap hydroelectric power provided by regional dams. While Spokane's residents welcome business and the jobs it arguably brings, they worry about how much pollution the air and especially the river can sustain. Studies show that there are 90 percent fewer fish in the river than there used to be, and that toxic chemicals in the river leach into aquifers, endangering the region's source of clean water. People are warned not to eat fish from the river, and the rate of contamination in breast milk is high.

Inadequate regulation and poor enforcement allow factories to pour toxins into the waters to such a degree that some scientists have compared the river to a terminally ill patient.

Shallan Dawson, a member of the Sierra Club's executive committee, is striving to protect the river she loves. According to Dawson, the Environmental Protection Agency considers toxic waste dumped into the river from upstream Idaho to be "natural background" rather than pollution. Adding insult to injury, Spokane residents are also dealing with phosphorus from local wastewater treatment plants being discharged into the river, causing heavy pollution.

SHALLAN DAWSON: It's so frustrating that the state's Department of Environmental Quality is ignoring its own studies and not enforcing the laws on the books.

In addition, during the summer months, to the chagrin of many local residents, the river gets "turned off" by dams upstream. This may add to the enjoyment of those who live on the lake upriver, and it may increase revenue from power production, but when the dam is opened up in the fall, tons of suspended toxins and heavy metals rush downstream. Federal agencies routinely preempt local control over related environmental issues. Recently, the Federal Regulatory Commission held hearings on the relicensing of dams owned by the energy company Avista.

Afterward, public discussion regarding the use of the dams was closed, by law, for fifty years.

Reframing the Problems in Democracy School

Breean Beggs was the director of the Center for Justice, a local non-profit law firm working to promote social justice in Spokane. He and Jim Sheehan, who is the founder of the center, had the opportunity to hear Thomas Linzey speak, and they invited him to teach Democracy School in their city.

JIM SHEEHAN: Our conversation had long revolved around the question: How do we make this place more democratic? Everyone has a voice, but do they have a forum, and how do we get a forum for people to be heard?

They were captivated by this new way of dealing with corporate powers, which teaches community members how to determine their own destiny through conversation and open decision making. Word of the school spread, and leaders from the neighborhood councils attended, as well as others who cared about Spokane.

BREEAN BEGGS: Democracy School taught me the history I didn't learn in law school. Corporate entities are meant to provide a public service, and, after the founding of our country, they were tightly controlled. They were meant to be tools of society, not considered as natural-born persons.

Another attendee was Brad Read, who had spent a lot of energy trying to get the city council to pass a number of nonbinding resolutions. At a certain point, he realized that these resolutions might make people feel good but were not enforceable law and were therefore ultimately meaningless. The school showed him why they needed enforceable law.

BRAD READ: I realized we've all gone through the same process with our organizing, which was about asking nicely and being denied, and realizing we don't have control.

Shallan Dawson found the school unsettling. It made her realize how much of her work with the Sierra Club had been essentially ineffective. At a recent meeting of the Sierra Club, the Environmental Protection Agency had agreed that the way water discharge permits for the Spokane River were formulated did not count toxic discharge from other states. But before the environmentalists could celebrate this decision, they learned that although new draft permits would soon go into effect, offending companies would be given ten additional years to meet the new standards. Dawson realized that company stakeholders had more rights than the people of Spokane.

SHALLAN DAWSON: I came to environmental protection with total idealism. I went to work doing river protection, being sure we would succeed, because people care, and they are willing to write letters and work harder and harder. But until you have enforceable law on the books, you won't see real improvement in water quality.

In Spokane, Democracy School did three things. First, it validated the idea that working through the regulatory system is a waste of time, as Dawson and others had clearly experienced. Second, it empowered individuals to realize they could create the community they wanted. As Patty Norton from Peaceful Valley observed: "It's hard to change the conversation from 'what can we get?' to 'what do we want?' We've been so beaten down, we were only focused on what little concessions we could get. Democracy School helps you change that conversation."

Finally, it demonstrated that individual rights at the local level are the most powerful tools for change available. As more schools were taught in the area, the community spirit became infectious; attendees began getting together to discuss what could be done in their city.

Out of these many conversations, Envision Spokane was born. The group quickly attracted a lot of people, including representatives from Spokane's neighborhood associations, community groups, churches, and labor unions, to discuss what they wanted for their city. While it started out as an envisioning exercise, the work transformed into a citywide campaign to rewrite Spokane's home rule charter—to drive legally enforceable rights for neighborhoods, people, workers, and nature directly into the structure of the city government itself. Envision Spokane asked CELDF to help them explore how this could be done.

Researching Spokane's Governing Structures

The city of Spokane makes decisions through a mayor-council form of government. Interestingly, it is also a "home rule city," which makes it attractive as a place for rights-based organizing. Municipal home rule began in the early twentieth century. Stimulated by what was called the progressive movement—which came into existence in response to government and corporate corruption and waste, and pushed reforms to give citizens more power over their own lives—it gave local citizens the right to adopt a charter for the community allowing them fundamental governing powers over local issues. Of course, under our present legal system, home rule can be trumped by state and federal laws.

BREEAN BEGGS: In the city charter, you have two opportunities to shift the balance: We can identify and expand the rights individuals have, and we can take back certain rights that have been granted to corporations.

The goal and aim of Envision Spokane is to literally rewrite the charter of the city by putting on the ballot a number of amendments for voters to consider.

Local Organizing Clusters

One challenge that arises in the process of organizing a city, as opposed to a small rural community, is the complexity and variety of interests presented by citizens. How do you create the possibility for so many different people to have input in the process? How do those already involved encourage a large amount of participation, so that they are representing everyone's concerns, yet also keep the process manageable? How do you realize a far-reaching intention that will require conversations numbering in the thousands?

The Envision Spokane participants, after establishing a permanent board, addressed this challenge by deciding to divide their members into three clusters: the neighborhood council cluster, the labor union cluster, and the community group cluster. The community group cluster included social justice advocacy, environmental organizations, and independent organizations such as business groups. Each cluster was invited to gather more participants to meet and discuss their vision for a bill of rights for the city of Spokane. This process was similarly painstaking and enlightening for each cluster, although different in particulars.

For Rick Evans of Laborers Local 238, who grew up in Spokane, the process was different from how he usually proceeds in his organizing: "We were being asked to make a wish list of what we would want as part of the Spokane charter. Normally we do top-down stuff like talking to owners of a company or setting up a picket line where job conditions are wrong. But working with Envision Spokane is more in tune with building coalitions."

The labor union cluster went through a process of prioritizing. Evans concluded that their final three proposed amendments reflected the makeup of those who were present the most.

That's how the democratic process works—you have to speak up if you want your voice to be heard. Nevertheless, as various unions were in discussion with each other during the negotiations, the amendments do represent the majority of common labor concerns. The cluster agreed on the right to be paid a living wage, the right to be paid the prevailing wage on construction projects, and the right to have constitutional protections within the workplace.

A consensus also began emerging in the neighborhood council cluster. The members prioritized seven concrete amendments all could agree on, although hammering out the precise language required a fair amount of effort. Rather than claiming the right to veto development projects, the group settled on the more general "right to determine their own futures." The group also determined it had the right for growth-related infrastructure costs to be provided by any new construction developments.

The community group cluster presented a wider array of concerns, including business-related issues, health care and housing issues, and questions about the environment. There was strong interest in providing greater rights to small businesses, which often have trouble accessing loans. To meet the goal of a sustainable city, it makes sense to find systemic ways to support local business so that the town is not dependent on national franchises, which don't have the same investment in the community.

Protecting the Spokane River from further damage was another thing easily agreed upon by everyone in the cluster. Participants followed the CELDF model and created an amendment to give nature a right to exist and to flourish. Their thinking was: If the Spokane River has rights, then individuals can speak on its behalf in order to protect it.

BREEAN BEGGS: We're a swing city politically, but everybody loves the river. As people have conversations about what they want to pass on to their grandchildren, they find common ground.

Mariah McKay, an articulate young activist, served as secretary to the community group cluster. She urged using the internet to get the word out as well as looking at other ways to get young people involved. She set up a website for Envision Spokane and did outreach through social media.

MARIAH McKAY: Developing and printing a flyer is expensive and laborious. We send out Envision Spokane meeting information with a Google alert. Organizing is like art. I would like Spokane to surprise everyone. The point is to enable ourselves to protect and secure the kind of lifestyle and future and environment that we want to be living in.

As it became clearer what the participants of each cluster wanted, the challenge became taking all those ideas and condensing them into to a reasonable set of proposals that could gain wide support and be voted into the city's charter.

Brad Read exuded great enthusiasm for the project: "This organizing is radically new. We are actually writing law, which is something this community has never undertaken before."

Should the city vote to pass the amendments, the Center for Justice has offered its legal staff to help enforce whatever rights Spokane has decided to place in its governing charter.

Spokane Bill of Rights

Residents have the right to a healthy, locally based economy.

Residents have the right to preventive health care.

Residents have the right to housing.

Residents have the right to a healthy environment.

The natural environment has the right to exist and flourish.

Neighborhoods have the right to determine their own futures.

Neighborhoods have the right to have growth-related infrastructure costs provided by new development.

Workers have the right to be paid a living wage, and if greater, to be paid the prevailing wage on construction projects.

Workers have the right to employer neutrality when unionizing and the right to constitutional protections within the workplace.

Workers have the right to work as apprentices on construction projects.

Residents, neighborhoods, workers, neighborhood councils, and the City of Spokane have the right to enforce these charter amendments.

Permanent Board Selects Charter Amendments

When the three clusters came back together as the Envision Spokane board, there were twenty-one proposed amendments between them. They realized that this number was too unwieldy to win approval by the general electorate. Each amendment was presented to the group in a briefing paper and then voted on to rank the top three from each cluster. Where there was clear overlap, the group was able to sign off relatively easily. The board ultimately agreed upon eleven proposals to constitute a bill of rights for the city charter, although the process of reconsidering and refining continued for another six months.

What They Learned

The process of coming together and hashing out the amendments for the final bill of rights was a truly rewarding experience for many participants. Of course, there were differences among each cluster's wishes. It would have been natural for the conflict to become heated as various parties pushed for the amendments they considered most crucial.

Everyone found that talking to each other and developing relationships not only circumnavigated this potential problem but also turned out to be the greatest part of the process.

Members often found themselves unwilling to stop their meeting at the appointed time and would still be there hours later, hashing out language and concepts.

Lois Irwin: We were all happy to meet others coming from different walks of life. We developed a sense of loyalty to one another and we learned from one another. These are the only meetings I've attended where I left feeling better than when I arrived.

Members of the board reported growing satisfaction as they got to know people from their city they didn't normally have the opportunity to meet. They were able to come to a deeper understanding of their fellow community members and the issues they faced and to learn more about the place they all inhabit.

Obstacles

As in many other cities, a few small groups have most of the power in Spokane. A major business family also owns the city newspaper, which means that major media is not necessarily on the side of Envision

Spokane. The Spokane utility corporation effectively owns the Spokane River. The organizers of Envision Spokane expected a strong pushback from these and other entrenched powers, anticipating that their efforts would be made to look silly, ridiculous, and even dangerous. To counteract this, they spread word of their message throughout the Web, and were pleased by the publication of a positive article in a weekly paper calling the group "cheerful rebels."

Another obstacle that activists faced was apathy. Many people still believe that those in power will come up with solutions to their problems. As well, many people are busy with their own lives and families, struggling to get by; for these people, participation in the larger life of the community may be overwhelming. Nor did all of Spokane's residents have the unusual opportunity to get together and discuss their opinions and issues. But the town hall process did offer the chance for proposals to be presented to large audiences throughout the city. This allowed the new proposals to be modified as an increasing number of Spokane residents had their voices heard. Some of these meetings were contentious, as, for example, some members of the chamber of commerce did not agree with the notion that local neighborhoods should have the power to stop new development.

Most compelling to those in Envision Spokane doing all the hard work was that, if their proposals passed, their amendments would become law. It would then be the responsibility of the city to enforce the provisions and remedy any of these new rights if they were violated.

Brad Read was excited for that day to come:

BRAD READ: It feels new because we don't usually focus on the part of our history where the abolitionists and suffragists changed illegitimate law. The only way they could do this was by doing the educational work it took to build a big enough movement.

The fundamental truth is deciding about who's in charge. When it comes to the decisions that affect your community and your children, and what the common future is going to look like, who gets to decide? If it's you, congratulations, you have democracy. If not, what are you going to do about it?

UPDATE: 2008–2016
Brad Read's dream of democracy has not yet come to pass.

In November 2009, the residents of the city of Spokane rejected the Bill of Rights. The vote was three to one against. The city tried to block the vote from being on the ballot and when that failed, posted advisory questions alongside the bill, suggesting city taxes would go up and services would go down as a result of implementing the Bill of Rights. In addition, much corporate campaign money was spent to defeat it. In spite of this, as Envision Spokane pointed out, one in four Spokane residents voted to radically change what government is about and whom it serves.

After the vote and its inevitable disappointment, what resonated most with the community were four planks in the Community Bill of Rights: neighborhoods, Spokane River, workers, and corporate power. So over the next year, Envision Spokane produced a new version of the Community Bill of Rights based in: Rights for Neighborhood residents to determine major development in their neighborhood, the Right to a healthy Spokane River and Aquifer, the Right for Constitutional Protections in the Workplace, and the Rights of People to not be Subordinated to Corporate Rights.

This time the city did not place advisory questions to accompany the ballot. Election night 2011 was exciting, as for a while it appeared that the Community Bill of Rights would be adopted. In the end it was narrowly defeated, with nearly thirty thousand people voting for the bill. Because Envision Spokane did not expect to get more than one third of the vote, they were pleased and heartened with the support the bill received. Organizers embraced how close they had come as a positive sign and started looking for what could be learned: to be oriented toward the longer term plan and to redefine short term failure as steps along the way.

Envision Spokane regrouped and in 2013 filed the same initiative with the four planks. While the city council declined to bring a pre-election challenge, a group of corporations did so instead—the local chamber of commerce, Spokane Homebuilders Association, Avista Utility Company, County Commissioners of Spokane County, and others. So before voters could weigh in, a Spokane County trial court judge ruled in August 2013 that the initiative lay beyond the power of the people to adopt at the municipal level, and blocked it from appearing on the ballot. At the same time the judge struck from the ballot an ordinance advanced by another group that would have banned corporate lobbying and electioneering.

The judge dealing with the Community Bill of Rights used substantive reasons to strike it from the ballot. Attorney Lindsey Schromen-Wawrin, who had worked with the earlier ballot initiative as a volunteer, came on board as the lawyer for Envision Spokane and on their behalf filed an emergency appeal, based on the corporate group not having standing to challenge the ballot initiative. Schromen-Wawrin's oral argument was heard in September 2014 in appellate court. Eventually, at the end of January 2015, this court ruled against this coalition of corporate challengers and the Community Bill of Rights went back on the ballot for the people of Spokane to decide on.

But the corporate interests appealed the ruling, and in November 2015 Lindsey Schromen-Wawrin gave the oral argument before the Washington Supreme Court. Envision Spokane lost that appeal unanimously in early 2016.

With the Community Bill of Rights kept from the ballot in 2013 and frozen by the glacial pace of the legal process, Envision Spokane reorganized to work on a new Community Rights ordinance. Aware of national attention to workers' rights issues around raising the minimum wage and a living wage as well as benefits like sick leave, Envision Spokane decided that a worker-specific bill of rights was the route to go.

BRAD READ: We wanted to deepen understanding and solidarity with those bread and butter struggles, and to disabuse folks of the idea that we just cared about environmental issues.

They formulated a bill of rights for workers, specifically: A right to a full family wage, a right to equal pay for equal work, a right to not be wrongfully terminated, and corporate rights do not trump workers' rights.

The Worker Bill of Rights faced the same issues as the 2013 Community Bill of Rights in the form of a pre-election legal challenge, this time from the mayor of Spokane. Unlike the earlier local judge, this judge found that initiatives are to be voted on by the people, and only if they pass, should the court have a role to play in terms of legality or constitutionality. Thus the Worker Bill of Rights got to be on the ballot. The city council, the majority being so-called liberals or progressives, counteracted the courtroom win for Envision Spokane by once again placing advisory questions to accompany the measure, suggesting that taxes would go up and city services go down if voters expanded these rights for workers.

A coalition of corporations spent over a quarter of a million dollars on media buys, direct mail, and yard signs, more than eight times as much as Envision Spokane spent on the whole campaign. They used the scare tactic that if workers' rights were passed, businesses would leave and nobody would have a job, turning Spokane into a ghost town. In November 2015, the Worker Bill of Rights was defeated, winning only 36 percent of the vote.

Redefining What a Win Means

Of course the loss at the polls was disappointing. But part of organizing is recognizing that failure is not the same as defeat, and redefining what a win means. They now know that groups need to look at how they build and maintain their resilience. Spokane's organizers have learned to respond to the various pushback moments. To build in the understanding that they would be attacked and that this attack will be used and that it takes time for this process to unfold. It has normalized those moments of attacks, because they clarify the situation local residents find themselves in, and they are then used as a springboard toward greater mobilization.

Moreover, Spokane has started to have an impact nationally as Envision Spokane has brought forward more than one Bill of Rights to serve as templates for other communities in other states to adopt. Organizers in Oregon and Colorado have learned from Spokane's process.

Given all that, how does Envision Spokane move forward? In February 2016, the Washington Supreme Court ruled against Envision Spokane and the initiative power, and Lindsey Schromen-Wawrin immediately filed a motion for reconsideration. The ruling not only permanently kicked the Community Bill of Rights off the ballot, but expanded judicial power to block any local initiative, of any kind, in the future, thereby eliminating direct democracy in communities across the state.

The group does not expect the motion to reconsider to change the outcome, so they will take some time to regroup and rebuild. That means finding new people, training and activating them to be the next wave of Envision Spokane, knowing full well the realities they are up against. The goal would be to build a more permanent presence with the political force to get the local bill of rights not just competing at the ballot box but adopted as the city charter. Alongside running local law campaigns the group will work to create more pressure on the elected bodies, the city council, or county commissioners.

The more the courts act to stonewall direct democracy locally, the more energy can be harnessed to work for changes needed at the state level that would then protect community rights at the local level. This is the next level of organizing; with the intent to start building a community rights people's party.

KAI HUSCHKE: It is now up to residents to push for the adoption of local self-government laws in places like Spokane, Bellingham, Seattle, Yakima, Ellensburg, Pullman, Olympia, Kettle Falls, and small and big towns in between, as the first major strides toward establishing something that many say has never existed in this country before—a true democracy.

Chapter 5
Colorado: From Local Lawmaking to Overhauling the State Constitution

FACED WITH MINING PROJECTS HARMFUL TO local environments and local economies, communities will rarely be able to depend on their elected state and local governments to protect their interests, as the billions of dollars at stake tend to purchase loyalty to the corporations rather than to the people they are supposed to represent. And, as we have seen, corporations have not only money and lobbyists on their side but a legal system hijacked by corporate rights. Therefore to be effective, citizens will have to step up their organizing to address that legal system directly.

Lafayette, Colorado: A Safe Place to Raise Children, but for How Long?

Lafayette is a home rule municipality situated north of Denver and east of Boulder, in Boulder County, with a population of around twenty-eight thousand people. It was founded in 1888, grew because of the coal mining boom and has a colorful history closely tied to coal mining and union organizing, once lending it a reputation as a union hotbed. According to the Lafayette town website, those tensions stopped for good when the last mine closed in 1957.

Nestled in the foothills just east of the Rocky Mountains, Lafayette boasts a network of parks, bikeways, wildlife corridors and habitats, plenty of outdoor recreation areas, and a strong sense of preservation of the natural beauty of the region. All of this attracted Cliff Willmeng and his family to relocate from Chicago in 2010. A year later, Cliff's mother, Merrily Mazza, who lived in Chicago and worked in educational publishing until she retired, purchased a little home a mile and a half away, close enough that the grandchildren could walk over. Mother and son were aware that the area northwest of Denver had been contaminated by plutonium waste products, so they were careful to not move downwind from Rocky Flats, and they felt lucky to have found their homes in such a beautiful and what they assumed was a protected environment.

One morning two years later, in June 2012, Cliff read in a local paper about a protest occurring in nearby Erie. He was struck by photos of picket signs against oil and gas wells in a community that clearly did not want this development. He and Merrily went to check out what was going on, and attended a meeting of concerned moms at the Erie Public Library. Encana corporation was about to install a fracking pad right next to Red Hawk Elementary School. A pad can host up to fifty-four wells.

Cliff's home in Lafayette is four miles away from this elementary school and in riding around, they realized that what they had assumed were ordinary water tanks dotting the East Boulder County landscape, were in actuality part of the fracking infrastructure. Only then did they learn they had bought their homes on the western edge of the Wattenberg shale formation, which is part of the larger Denver Julesberg Basin shale formation. No chamber of commerce or other city informational website mentioned this in their PR, their position being that the oil and gas industry is not interested in Lafayette.

While drilling for oil is not new to the area, hydraulic fracturing is. Erie's board listened to the residents' objections but gave the go ahead to Encana. Cliff and Merrily met a number of women who had spent months fighting this development and every single one ended up moving away from Erie when they realized that their voice carried no weight. The pad went up six months later.

Merrily Mazza: I already had the background to understand how the system is rigged. I come from the corporate side, and worked for a textbook company where I read financial reports, including the money spent on lobbying. I got to see how "No Child Left Behind" was a moneymaker for the textbook companies.

At the same time they saw that more and more communities were getting wells right next to their houses. As a registered nurse, and the father of young children, Cliff was concerned about the dangers of toxic chemicals, so he started to do some research. He discovered that Dr. John Hughes, a local doctor had collected serum samples from folks to test for volatile organic compounds. Every subject from Erie came back positive for high amounts of the cancer-causing benzene and three other harmful chemicals. Cliff and his mother started to view the issue of fracking as an issue of life and death.

MERRILY MAZZA: Really, it's like putting a chemical plant right next door to your home. It's crazy. You can't have a fireworks factory in your garage but you can place these wells in the middle of residential areas. Our neighboring communities are a sacrifice zone for the oil and gas industry.

CLIFF WILLMENG: If we don't have the right to defend our community against such dangers, we don't have rights at all.

East Boulder County United Gets Started

Cliff and Merrily's first actions that summer in 2012 were to find other concerned community members. Over the next months, they grew from four people to over a dozen committed members and called themselves East Boulder County United. The group communicated with the Lafayette City Council, expressing their concern that oil and gas development would compromise life in their little town. To their surprise, the city council told them that they were unaware of such development, as they don't deal with questions about oil and gas. The mayor actually told Cliff that there were few if any active wells in Lafayette, but in fact there are fourteen. In addition, they said that there was nothing they could do to prohibit development and suggested the concerned residents go to the state legislature to find a remedy. So that's what they did.

Their state representative, Mike Foote, was honest. He told them point blank that nothing the oil industry would object to would pass the legislature.

Panic ensued. The group sat down to craft a strategy that would keep Lafayette safe. One member who joined the group was Dr. Tom Groover, who had met one of the kids sent home sick in Erie. This anti-GMO activist did not need to be told about the system being rigged. When he spoke at the public hearings, it was evident that the Boulder County commissioners had already made up their minds. While there's no fracking in his immediate neighborhood, Groover knew there were already twenty-five thousand wells just east and northeast of him and that the industry wanted to bring in more. Discouraged, he attended a Democracy School and found a kindred soul in Cliff Willmeng.

At that time the larger town to their north, Longmont, was campaigning for a ban on fracking. East Boulder County United was inspired by the idea of an outright ban instead of regulating harm in parts per million, so they decided to support this campaign. Even though the campaign ran into threats by state government and companies and even though Longmont's city council would not support the ban, nevertheless, the ballot initiative won in November 2012 with 60 percent of the vote. In early 2013, however, they got sued by the Colorado Oil and Gas Association. The Longmont ban was found to be illegal by Judge D.D. Mallard and thrown out.

As East Boulder County United debated the problem, some wanting a ban on fracking in Lafayette's city limits, others to work on passing a moratorium, a woman who worked for nonprofits brought up CELDF. They got Ben Price and Thomas Linzey on the phone and the core group of East Boulder County United was introduced to a rights-based approach. Unfamiliar with CELDF, Cliff did not trust in legal firms. In vigorous discussion among group members, eventually the question was asked: "What do you want?" "What are we entitled to as community members?" As in other communities across the country, this question proved transformative.

CLIFF WILLMENG: We began to realize how much bigger this was than simply regulating fracking. And so our vision became bigger for what we needed to accomplish.

So East Boulder County United decided they wanted to have a bill of rights to protect Lafayette, but they also decided to do more than that, to initiate a larger grassroots movement in order to address the privilege the fossil fuel companies enjoy. Such privilege goes far back in Colorado. In his research Cliff came upon the failure of the cyanide ban in the 1990s, when a Canadian mining corporation's use of cyanide poisoned the water table. At that time five counties tried to protect their residents' health by passing laws forbidding the use of cyanide, but the Colorado Supreme Court decided that the use of cyanide could not be banned, because it would *violate the rights of the mining company to obtain their mineral resources*. Thus the group knew of the precedent of preemption by the state of local laws enacted to protect the health and safety of the community. With that in mind, and with the help of Ben's suggestions, they started to write their own Bill of Rights.

A Lafayette Bill of Rights

The Lafayette Bill of Rights establishes community rights to self-governance, rights to clean air and water, freedom from chemical trespass, the right to sustainable energy future and rights of ecosystems. It bans all new oil and gas development, new infrastructure, and waste disposal. In order to protect those rights, the bill bans projects and laws that protect those projects, such as corporate personhood, at the same time. Part 2 bans all gas drilling as a violation of those rights. (See Appendix.)

In the summer and fall, East Boulder County United gathered two thousand signatures to place the initiative on the ballot. The Lafayette City Council opposed this effort and within weeks the effort was also challenged by an individual from the town who worked for Halliburton and had the backing of a legal firm hired by the oil and gas association. East Boulder County United members went door to door, canvassing around fracking and the larger issue of rights, and with the help of CELDF made sure their bill met legal requirements.

Because the city council opposed the bill, the group realized that if they won, they would need to have people on city council to enforce the measure. So they ran two candidates for city council, one of them Merrily.

MERRILY MAZZA: It was a lot of work but not difficult. I knocked on doors. I talked to groups, like the local League of Women Voters. I found much concern about fracking, but still people needed to be educated because the oil and gas industry pays for good PR, running ads on TV presenting themselves as high-tech nontoxic job creators.

In November 2013 Merrily and the ballot initiative won by 60 percent of the vote. At the same time the city council's two most vocal members against the ballot were defeated. Within a month, in December, the Colorado Oil and Gas Association sued Lafayette under Colorado law, challenging the Bill of Rights on the principle that a municipal government has no authority to ban oil and gas activity, only the state can do that, and therefore Lafayette had exceeded its authority. The same suit also cited Broomfield and Fort Collins for passing a five-year moratorium.

MERRILY MAZZA: They present themselves as the good guys, but look at what the oil and gas companies are saying to the city officials: we will bankrupt your community if you try to stop us. And the city officials beg the regulatory commission for tiny concessions to support the concerns of their residents, but the reality is that the council has little power

The Lafayette City Council had been warned, it was something they were expecting, and while a few grumbled, they voted to defend the suit. Merrily did have to recuse herself from those votes, and she had to resign from the board of EBCU as it presented a conflict of interest.

Addressing the Lawsuit

Enter Libby Comeaux, at the time a retired lawyer, taking a break to deal with family issues. She had worked in the state administrative system and seen the influence of corporate America first hand, and when she heard Thomas Linzey speak, realized the problem was not particular to that agency, but systemic. The year before, in 2012, she had hosted a conference, *The Downstream Neighbor*, centered on water as an intrinsic right and public trust. She invited scholars, activists, and contemplatives, and had been inspired to learn about CELDF's rights-of-nature work.

Libby Comeaux: Over the years I had found the practice of law less and less in touch with reality; it's based in Newtonian mechanics and not adapting to our current knowledge of the natural world.

A working group spun off from the Democracy School and Libby, an obsessive note-taker, naturally became the secretary when they started setting up the state network. She had no intention of practicing again, but once she saw that Lafayette's law needed legal defense, she stepped up to represent East Boulder County United in the lawsuit that the Colorado Oil and Gas Association has filed against the city of Lafayette. Renewing her license wasn't difficult, but as she had never practiced this kind of appellate law, she was on a steep learning curve.

The people of Lafayette who adopted the community rights ordinance, knowing that the city would not defend the ordinance on the basis of the people's right to pass it, attempted to intervene in the case, but were denied by the court. In addition to appealing the denial of intervention, Cliff and another resident of Lafayette filed a class action lawsuit against the Colorado Oil and Gas Association (COGA) and the state of Colorado, for denying the right of the people of Lafayette to local, community self-government.

As predicted by the people of Lafayette, the city failed to defend the ordinance in a way that asserted the right of the people to adopt it, and the District Court hearing the case by COGA against Lafayette ruled in favor of COGA. The city council then refused to appeal the loss.

Organizing at the State Level

Back in December 2013, fresh off the win of the ballot and realizing that it would take changes to state law to help communities defend themselves, East Boulder County United reached out to educate other communities, bringing Ben Price and Thomas Linzey to speak on several occasions. From this effort the Colorado Community Rights Network (COCRN) was born. The members of COCRN meet monthly and hold summits throughout the state, with several hundred active participants, including lots of folks from Denver.

This group decided to push for structural changes in the state constitution because the only way to protect their communities was to affect state-level change and such change would cover a number of issues because the underlying root cause is the same. Whether the issue is GMO agricultural contamination or community toxic waste dumping or mining or unwanted development or fracking or the fight for a living wage, each of these problems has in common the need to push for local democratic decision-making power at the state level.

Thomas Linzey believes this surge of activism occurred partly because the state was a direct enforcer of the unjust law and came in to sue the community. It is a powerful teaching moment the first time a state directly intervenes, which clarifies for many that the enemy is not just the corporation but the state as its enforcer. Many saw that what was most needed was an amendment to the state constitution that would legalize community rights.

DR. TOM GROOVER: The state wants to argue that they alone have a right to regulate what happens in our communities but we need to get the argument to be about community rights and rights for nature. And we want to make it contagious, to have a people's movement.

So in January 2014 COCRN filed a Petition to put the "Colorado Community Rights Amendment" to the state constitution on the ballot. They worked hard to refine the language through a number of drafts, expressing their intent in as inspirational a manner as possible. (See Appendix.) The ballot initiative was approved by the state board, but shortly thereafter it was challenged by the Colorado Chamber of Commerce and the Colorado Mining Association. Although the Colorado Supreme Court eventually ruled in COCRN's favor, because the legal challenges restricted the window of time for signature gathering to around nine weeks, COCRN failed to get enough signatures in 2014 and therefore resubmitted the measure in 2015.

One question that is often raised is how such an amendment might weaken other protections in place. COCRN and other state organizations doing rights-based work explain that the amendment authorizes people within localities to adopt local bills of rights, which expand and increase constitutional rights and protections while prohibiting communities from restricting or constricting currently recognized state and federal constitutional rights.

As they make sure is clear, the proposed amendment doesn't specifically prohibit fracking. Any community is free to allow it if they want it. Once it gets on the ballot and the people of Colorado get to vote, if it passes, lawsuits like the one against Lafayette will be a thing of the past.

Coalition-Building as Part of Organizing

To build interest and support for the state amendment, Cliff Willmeng has taken a presentation called "Legalizing Democracy Where We Live" all over Colorado, telling the story of Lafayette, their ordinance, and inviting other communities to join in. He shows a Colorado map, covered in red dots representing fifty-five thousand oil and gas wells, twenty-two thousand in Weld County alone. The fracking issue draws a lot of attention but it's also Cliff's intention to broaden the coalition pushing for change. His presentations fill venues and draw intense conversation. Groups with varying concerns have joined in to endorse the amendment: people fighting GMOs and pesticides, 15 NOW—fighting for a living wage, Metro Denver Community Rights, Toxic Free Lafayette, Windsor Community Rights Network, DU Divestment group, Bee Safe Boulder, Move to Amend, Loretto community, Chris Hedges, Colorado Green Party, and others.

CLIFF WILLMENG: The amendment disrupts preemption by granting local governments a constitutional right to raise state standards—empowering them to boost the minimum wage, bolster environmental protections, and strengthen tenant rights, for example. It would recognize the authority of local governments "to enact local laws that protect health, safety and welfare by recognizing or establishing rights of natural persons, their local communities and nature."

Sometimes Merrily goes with Cliff, but often she goes to present in places where her status as a city councilor will carry some weight, for instance the Democratic Party. The Lafayette City Council voted to endorse the state ballot initiative, as has the Democratic Party of Denver. It's less easy to build coalitions with some of the environmental and liberal nonprofits, as they still believe this process for driving change is too radical.

What Cliff and Merrily and the other members of East Boulder County United find most challenging in their organizing work is convincing their fellow citizens they are wasting their time talking to the state legislature. It's hard to rip off that veil. Denial is a hard nut to crack.

Merrily Mazza: They don't yet get that we need to lead our legislators. People need to believe that the system is fair, that if they follow the right procedure and appeal to the right people and agency, that they will be listened to. To question that state of affairs, you have to question everything. It's hard for people to accept that we were lied to and it's all about money. If you stop believing we live in a democracy, then what?

Legal Shenanigans

COCRN's Community Rights amendment was challenged first in 2014 by the Chambers of Commerce and the Mining Association. Libby and COCRN eventually won that challenge at the Supreme Court. However, those legal shenanigans took so much time, they spent a year regrouping and now are beginning to contact counties all over again. In August 2015, they started preparing to campaign to get enough signatures to appear on the ballot in November 2016. And COCRN continued to spend time and energy jumping through the hoops of the State vetting process. One final hoop involved Comeaux writing the brief to defend COCRN before the Supreme Court to the latest objection by the American Petroleum Institute in 2016.

Comeaux explains that the initiative process has many hurdles designed to protect the public from being defrauded, which has yielded a huge body of case law. The initiative must address one single subject and the title must be clear and accurate so you can know what you are voting for. But there are lots of ways you can lose without it being about the actual issue. Those with a corporate agenda are not trying to protect those on the street who might be fooled, as they claim; instead they are wielding case law to keep the initiative off the ballot. In spite of which, Comeaux and COCRN succeeded in getting the ballot language approved by the Colorado Supreme Court on March 10, 2016.

COCRN hopes to get 150,000 signatures by August 2016, which are needed in order to produce some 99,000 vetted signatures. As a totally volunteer effort, this will present a huge challenge

MERRILY MAZZA: It's a hell of a lot of work. I'm fortunate in that I don't have financial pressures. I do this because I have grandchildren and they have to grow up in this world.

CLIFF WILLMENG: The potential is here because the Colorado Community Rights Amendment fuses all of this stuff together, and you've got a lot more tributaries starting to lead in. It's not just about fracking, it's rent control, it's cyanide use, it's the local living wage, it's all of that stuff that is about whether we have a collective future.

***

Be It Enacted by the People of the State of Colorado

In the constitution of the state of Colorado, **add** section 32 to article II as follows:

Section 32. Right of Local Community Self-Government

(1) As all political power is vested in and derived from the people, and as all government of right originates from the people, the people have an inherent and inalienable right of local community self-government in each county, city, town, and other municipality.

(2) That right shall include the power of the people, and the power of their governments, to enact local laws that protect health, safety, and welfare by recognizing or establishing rights of natural persons, their local communities, and nature; and by securing those rights using prohibitions and other means deemed necessary by the community, including measures to establish, define, alter, or eliminate competing rights, powers, privileges, immunities, or duties of corporations and other

business entities operating, or seeking to operate, in the community.

(3) Notwithstanding section 16 of article XIV or section 6 of article XX of this constitution, local laws adopted pursuant to subsection (2) of this section shall not be subject to preemption or nullification by international, federal, or state laws, provided that:

    (a) Such local laws do not restrict fundamental rights of natural persons, their local communities, or nature secured by local, state, or federal constitutions, or by international law; and

    (b) Such local laws do not weaken protections for natural persons, their local communities, or nature provided by state, federal, or international law.

(4) All provisions of this section are self-executing and severable.

Chapter 6

Oregon and Ohio: Ordinances Pave the Way for Community Rights Networks

Organizing in Oregon

In the fall of 2011, a group called GMO Free Oregon reached out to CELDF to draft a Community Bill of Rights banning GMOs in Oregon. That draft law, although never run at the state level, was picked up by farmers in Benton County. Home to many farmers, Benton County is located in the Willamette Valley and is the birthplace to the first organic certifying standards in the U.S. The county's seat and main city, Corvallis, is the home of Oregon State University, which receives large amounts of funding from Monsanto Company for GMO research. A group of long-time local food system defenders in Benton County organized to deal with the growing threat of GMOs and the failure of the regulatory system to protect the health of sustainable agriculture. Decades of fighting unsustainable agricultural practices including GMOs within the system brought these activists to a rights-based approach that would legalize sustainable agriculture.

Banning GMOs

It all started at a meeting on March 10, 2012, with a presentation for farmers and representatives of the food community from eight Oregon counties. One of the first activists to get involved was Dana Allen, a former accountant and current farmer, owner of Rebel Farms, specializing in edible greens, flowers, and hydroponics and working with farmers' markets. She is passionate about seeds as the source of life. "In Corvallis we're focused on local food and food as the basis of community," she declares.

"When local food dies, community dies." Dana attended a meeting hosted by Oregon activist Paul Cienfuegos.

DANA ALLEN: The thing that hooked us was the sample food bill of rights. Paul had us each read a paragraph out loud. When it was my turn, I got too choked up to continue. I was so moved, I felt, this is it.

At the end of the presentation, they met in county-specific groups, and six from Benton County decided on the spot they were going to take on community rights work. The Benton County Community Rights coalition was launched and began to draft a countywide food bill of rights to ban GMOs. They filed their first petition with the county in October 2012 for placement of the initiative on the ballot. Meeting every Monday at 5 p.m. at the New Morning Bakery in Corvallis, they invited Kai Hushke, CELDF's Northwest Organizer from Spokane, Washington, to assist on the organizing front. Learning what was going on in Spokane got them grounded and prepared for what they would be facing. Spokane was inspirational as they were prepared for pushback, even if the exact form of that pushback wasn't known.

The Benton group spent months reworking the original draft of the ordinance they received from CELDF, putting it through many iterations.

DANA ALLEN: We owned and stood by every word and would go on to stand up for the essence of this food bill of rights through court battles and assaults by the corporations and the current system. Kai didn't tell us how to write it but instead helped us by asking us to clarify our intent. Formulating the intent section of the ordinance was deeply emotional, it allowed us to recognize what motivates us to spend years of our lives doing this work.

That fall and winter, CELDF Democracy Schools were held in Eugene and Corvallis. Among the participants was Michelle Holman, a woodworker who has made a living making educational kids' puzzles, and an avid back-to-the-lander whose garden produces five hundred jars of canned produce a year. Just as it did with Dana, the idea of community rights resonated at such a deep level that she immediately helped launch Community Rights Lane County. This strong core group has been meeting every Monday for the past three and a half years.

Another participant who lives in Eugene is Ann Kneeland, an attorney with a background in social and environmental justice. Over the next year she would be instrumental in doing all the legal work involved in getting a number of rights-based laws passed or on the ballot, among them three Lane County Community Rights ordinances.

Other Counties Come on Board

As the Lane County group was at work writing an ordinance to ban aerial spraying of pesticides, they saw Benton County doing ordinance work to stop GMOs and realized there was a huge conversation nationally on GMOs. It made sense to use that energy for a local food bill of rights. They shelved the spray ordinance and began drafting and organizing around their countywide food bill of rights ordinance that would prohibit GMOs.

In March 2013, the Willamette Farm and Food Rights Summit was held near Corvallis with activists from eight counties, and this boosted and strengthened the work and support for Benton and Lane Counties in trying to pass their food bills of rights.

That fall, a third county to get interested in this rights-based approach was Josephine County, where the Freedom from Pesticides Alliance wanted to remove pesticide use in the timber industry. They were first out of the starting gate with a bill of rights that would prohibit governmental, commercial, and industrial pesticide use. They filed their ordinance in the fall of 2013, and their petition was approved for circulation, as was the Benton County ordinance. Unlike those judges, the Lane County judge denied the petition, stating the ordinance had too many components. At the same time two other Oregon counties, facing a natural gas pipeline and export terminal, started talking about the right to a sustainable energy future.

From Corvallis to State Amendment

Riding this wave of organizing, in September 2013, folks from eight counties came together to formulate the Corvallis Declaration of Community Rights. Herein representatives from those counties declared their rights of local community self-government and their authority to stop corporate harms. Based in the Declaration of Independence, it calls on the people of Oregon to enact local laws that recognize community rights and ecosystem rights, to challenge through those laws the system of law that secures greater rights to corporations than residents, and to build a statewide network to change the Oregon Constitution. The document was signed by movers and shakers from eight different counties.

DANA ALLEN: The Corvallis Declaration is our foundational document. It's inspirational. And it created palpable energy toward statewide action.

So in the winter of 2014, the Oregon Community Rights Summit gathered in Eugene to formally launch the Oregon Community Rights

Network (ORCRN). This network of local groups formed a council of delegates, signed bylaws and decided to launch a state constitutional amendment campaign to recognize the right of local community self-government.

In the state of Oregon, unlike in states like Pennsylvania and New Hampshire, where one has to go through state legislatures, the constitution can be directly amended by state voters. In the beginning of 2015, ORCRN started work on the language of the statewide amendment and for the organizing campaign that would support the amendment. ORCRN's Right of Local Community Self-Government state constitutional amendment was then filed with the secretary of state, along with its sponsorship signatures. Oregon was the second state in the Union, after Colorado, to file such an amendment. At the same time Oregonians for Community Rights (O4CR) was formed as the political organization to run the state amendment campaign.

Meanwhile, in the summer of 2014, other counties became active in regards to the issues that most concerned them: Lincoln County filed a Freedom from Pesticides Bill of Rights to ban aerial spraying. Columbia, Coos, and Douglas Counties each filed a bill of rights for a sustainable energy future . . . a future that prohibits such things as pipelines coming through. Attorney Ann Kneeland has been busy representing folks in Benton County in court two different times. She represented the people in Columbia, Douglas, and Coos Counties supporting the ban on aerial

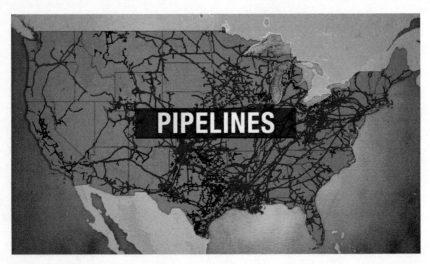

Map of oil and gas pipelines in the United States.

spraying on February 29, 2016. In addition she's involved in the legal issues surrounding the state amendment campaign.

ANN KNEELAND: This is the best place I can put my energy. We can't just sit back. I have a young son and I have fear for the future.

Pushback: They Don't Win Until You Go Home

In November 2014, Josephine County's Freedom from Pesticides Bill of Rights was voted on, and was defeated with 65 percent of the vote. Given that timber and big agriculture run the state of Oregon, and there was a bare minimum of an organized campaign, the result was actually inspiring. Moreover and more importantly, while they lost at the polls, this challenge shifted a larger part of the conversation to the idea of rights. Also, it provided a learning curve, as organizing a voting campaign isn't the same as drafting the ordinance with a small group of committed people. Educating voters about what the ordinance means is not an easy sound-bite kind of task.

In May 2015, the Benton County Food Ordinance was also defeated in the election by a decent margin, in no small thanks to industrial agriculture and chemical corporations. There was great disappointment among the local activists, but it was also a powerful learning experience that brought the lessons learned from Spokane to bear.

DANA ALLEN: I can remember sitting in my car and telling CELDF organizer Kai Huschke we got shot down. I felt like my baby's leg was shot off. But I came to understand that this was part of the process. We keep getting up. This child from Benton County may not have made it, but the Lane Community Rights ban on GMOs ordinance grew out of the one in Benton, and there are a lot more siblings being born all over Oregon too.

Kai Huschke was able to support the Oregon groups through the process with wisdom gained from Spokane. What Spokane taught is that pushback will happen and you have to be prepared for it. They can predict, to a large degree, in what form pushback will happen and that gives reasons to trust the work because they know how to respond. They also know that groups need to look at how they build and maintain their resilience over the long haul.

Changing broader structures takes time. The folks in Benton learned from Spokane to think longer-term and this created resiliency as part of the original mindset. They were able to build in the understanding that they would be attacked and that such attacks clarify the situation we the people find ourselves in. Those attacks are used as a springboard toward greater mobilization and this process takes time to unfold. It also helps in reducing fear around civil disobedience.

MICHELLE HOLMAN: This path makes sense, and it's also good for my growth. I get to practice patience, to do a lot of deep breathing, as I get so annoyed with the complacency of people.

DANA ALLEN: Right now the Benton County crew is resting up, and we've gone to the next level, getting other community rights chapters off the ground, focusing on the state constitutional amendment.

Next Phase of Organizing

The Constitutional Amendment to Secure the Right of Local Community Self-Government was officially filed in February 2015. That triggered a mini petitioning phase, in which they gathered one thousand signatures before submitting it to the Oregon attorney general for review in May 2015. Deciding that the amendment failed to meet the single subject requirement imposed by the state constitution, the secretary of state and attorney general refused to allow the petition to be circulated for signature gathering.

With CELDF's help, ORCRN members examined the state's reasoning and concluded that the state was mistaken, but instead of challenging the state, they made the decision to tinker with the amendment language, with CELDF's guidance, to produce a new version to strengthen enforceability. The new version was filed in the fall of 2015, and ORCRN was successful in once again gathering the thousand signatures, which again activated the review process from the secretary of state.

ANN KNEELAND: This is how it is with court proceedings: they are slow, dull, negative, off-putting to most people, and this is exactly what the system is trying to do, grind people down by drawing cases out. It's a strategy to dim the enthusiasm for creating change. That means it's even more important to our movement to stay connected to our hearts, because at the root, it's about our humanity.

At the very same time Lincoln County's Bill of Rights passed the administrative review from the county clerk, the Columbia County's Right to a Sustainable Energy Future ordinance was approved for petition circulation, Lane County approved the Local Food System Charter Amendment, and Douglas County's clerk approved the Right to a Sustainable Energy Future ordinance, the step before approval for petition circulation.

While these individual counties continue their active efforts to pass local ordinances into law, at the state level, if there's no obstruction from state or corporate interests, if there's zero legal challenge, at the end of March 2016, ORCRN will start gathering 140,000 signatures. However, because the group anticipates being stuck in court and not being able to qualify for 2016, they intend to use this time to put a longer term strategy in place for the 2018 election. This includes education and outreach to other communities and organizations.

They intend to organize more events with a statewide draw, like the summits. In November 2016 they are bringing Winona LaDuke to the University of Oregon to speak and to participate in a rights of nature working group.

MICHELLE HOLMAN: CELDF's work is great in that it transcends political stripes, but we need more people of color and marginalized folks. After all, who understands better than marginalized people what corporations are doing? I also think it would help to lose the "environmental" label. This is about rights; it's about justice.

In regards to building support and momentum, aside from fostering coalitions with more local groups, ORCRN aims to activate individuals out there who are not yet involved, extending their outreach to larger Oregon communities like Salem and Portland. In Portland there are lots of issues but not one unifying issue for the city, so activists haven't coalesced around a threat to move the work forward.

Dana Allen feels like the work is at a tipping point. CELDF has kept expanding the legal side of things but now it's about learning and evolving the organizing side. The Democracy School is great at educating people but that doesn't necessarily activate campaigns, and that is what needs to happen and is happening in Oregon.

DANA ALLEN: It's not just about passing the bill; it's about supporting the bill. The initiatives are important, for sure protecting our community and agriculture is important, but the real purpose of doing this work is supporting the movement, organizing one community at a time.

Organizing in Ohio

In Ohio, as in Oregon, community rights work has spread with relative speed. In 2012, three municipalities adopted Community Bills of Rights, namely Broadview Heights, Yellow Springs, and Mansfield. Oberlin passed their ordinance through initiative in 2013, and Athens in 2014. Five other communities are in various states of the process: Bowling Green, Gates Mills, Niles, Kent, and Youngstown, the latter now on its sixth try to pass their Community Bill of Rights. In addition there are five counties organizing to pass countywide community rights home rule charters, with two counties already in the signature gathering phase for the 2016 election cycle.

Unlike in Oregon, where a number of different issues are driving the activism, all these communities began organizing to protect themselves against the same threat, that of hydraulic fracturing, its compressor stations, its wastes, and the pipelines that service the industry. Pipelines may be deceptively sold as "utilities" to the public; in reality they are used to transport fossil fuels for export and profit. And far from safe as touted, federal records in 2014 showed pipeline leaks, spills, and incidents at the rate of nearly one a day.

Broadview Heights and Youngstown

In Broadview Heights, Ohio, a residential community near Cleveland that has been her home since childhood, Tish O'Dell became aware of the dangers of fracking in 2010, when she was attending a city council meeting on an unrelated issue and a woman named Susan stood up and accused the council of poisoning her children. A company called Cutter Oil, known for having a dismal safety record with lots of violations, had mowed down the trees behind her house and started drilling as, unbeknownst to her, they owned the mineral rights to her half-acre lot. The city said there was nothing they could do to protect her children against the noise, or against the toxic pollution of her air and water.

This woman's impassioned plea struck a deep chord in O'Dell. Over the years she had been employed in the local school district as a career specialist, working with kids, K through 12, and had been dismayed by the huge increase of kids with cancer and autism since she attended school as a youngster.

TISH O'DELL: Pollution is rampant. I come from immigrant grandparents who grew their food themselves and so I learned early that you don't poop where you eat. Since their time, I have experienced a lot of cancer in my family. The answer isn't building more cancer centers, but stopping the flow of untold thousands of toxic and cancer-causing chemicals into our water, our soil, our air.

She followed the same trajectory as had Cliff and Merrily Mazza in Colorado. She complained to the city council, who told her go to the state. She met with her state representative and senator, went to the Ohio EPA, and was sent into that same regulatory loop that she realized was leading nowhere. She learned that in 2004 the state passed a preemption bill to allow drilling in Ohio whether the people wanted it or not. Poking around in financial reports, she was not surprised to find that several city councilmembers received money from the gas industry. She decided to run for mayor in 2011, and although she lost the election, she met many other concerned residents. Showing the documentary *Gasland* at a campaign event, she was confronted by an angry, concerned mother, Michelle Aini. Although they got off to a confrontational start, they soon realized that they were on the same side, and within a few months O'Dell and Aini cofounded a local group called Mothers Against Drilling In Our Neighborhood (MADION).

Over in eastern Ohio, in Youngstown, a city with a population of around sixty-five thousand, where deep drilling rights had been sold to Chesapeake Energy in 2010, fracking wells were appearing all over the city. There Susie and Ray Beiersdorfer, geologists who grew up and worked in the oil and gas fields in California, were raising their twin girls while teaching geology, she in high school and he at the university. On December 31, 2011, they experienced a 4.0 magnitude earthquake. Susie was downtown in a deli when the window glass shook; it felt to her like a truck running into the building. Seismic stations have shown 566 seismic events for one well, DNL Northstar #1. The Ohio Department of Natural Resources claimed there was no correlation between the fracking activity and the earthquakes, but that mistaken claim has since been proven wrong. Having geologists on the team makes it harder to fool people.

With a few other concerned residents, the Beiersdorfers formed FrackFree Mahoning Valley. Members of this group kept going to township and other community meetings trying to educate their fellow Youngstown residents; they presented at the city council, they designed educational forums and brought in speakers, they did all the things people are supposed to do to try to protect their neighborhood and city, but their council kept voting to allow more drilling. Susie Beiersdorfer even ran for president of the city council as the Green Party candidate and came in second against the former mayor. It wasn't until a frack well was being drilled in their drinking water protection area of Meander Reservoir, in 2012, that a critical mass of folks were motivated to try a rights-based approach.

SUSIE BEIERSDORFER: Apathy is the enemy which is most easily overcome by a disaster in our face, because it's only then that people start to realize that the state agencies are not taking care of them, and they start to wake up.

Another such motivating spark has been lit by the harm being done to Mill Creek Park, a large metro park beloved by Youngstown residents fifteen miles south of town. Deep drilling rights on people's property abutting the park had been sold to Chesapeake Energy, and slant wells were drilled in the 1980s. More recently a new executive director fired the horticulturalist and naturalist who had provided good stewardship of the park for years, is putting in a fancy golf course, and in the paperwork has listed logging and gas development under "recreational activities." A Sunoco gas pipeline was laid, a sewer line was breached, and in the three park lakes fed by the Mahoning River, all the fish died. This kind of harm and mismanagement is emblematic of what the people of Ohio are up against, and it is fueling the fight for local control.

Communities Contact CELDF

Over in Broadview Heights, Tish O'Dell and MADION learned about CELDF and contacted Ben Price. Excited by what they learned, they tried to educate their seven-member city council about what the Community Bill of Rights could do for them. They invited Doug Shields, the city councilman who had successfully spearheaded the Community Bill of Rights that banned fracking in Pittsburgh, to come speak. Many residents were heartened by his inspirational talk but not so the city council. The members listened and told the residents to go ahead and draft an ordinance for Broadview Heights, stringing the group along for months, then roundly rejected the bill when it finally came up for a vote. MADION members felt shocked and betrayed by their elected representatives when the bill did not pass.

In Ohio there is the constitutional right to propose laws by initiative petitioning. Like most of us, O'Dell didn't know how to exercise her right to petition, and discovered that often the board of elections doesn't even know or else gives out the wrong information. So O'Dell and her colleagues engaged in a steep learning process, with Ben Price guiding them long-distance in how to do a petition by the people. To attract attention to their effort and educate residents about the Community Bill of Rights and the dangers of fracking, the group held panel discussions, inviting medical and other experts, a state representative who was concerned about drilling in neighborhoods, and even someone from a drilling company.

TISH O'DELL: We started signature gathering in front of the library, the post office, city hall; we walked the neighborhoods in extremely hot temperatures that lasted even after the sun went down. We needed 1,300 valid signatures to get on the ballot but gathered 1,900 to be safe. It's so much work, and then it hits you how easy it is for corporations to get laws passed: their lobbyist just walks over to the government official's office and delivers the law they want passed with campaign contribution in hand. For people to pass a law or amend one is a hundred times harder.

After collecting the necessary signatures, O'Dell and her core group started to campaign to get people to vote for it. That entailed a lot more work. "People always want to make everything a partisan issue, but our yard signs, 'Vote for Issue 29,' stood next to both Romney and Obama signs," O'Dell was pleased to notice. She was more pleased when in November the Community Bill of Rights Charter Amendment passed in Broadview Heights by 67 percent. There has been no new drilling in the community, and the wells already present are producing less and less. The group's success has been duplicated by four other Ohio municipalities so far, with five others in the process.

The residents of Youngstown, however, were not so fortunate. The Youngstown Community Bill of Rights Committee, which emerged from the group FrackFree Mahoning Valley, placed the Community Bill of Rights on the ballot for the first time in May 2013 and lost the vote after doing all the same work of collecting signatures and educating the public, but this did not stop the campaign. The committee, consisting of five or six committed people, continued to organize and mount campaigns year after year. The initiative has been on the ballot in every election since then, and is losing by less and less of the vote. They have been outspent, they have not received one official endorsement, and the Democratic Party sent around flyers urging people to vote no. But they keep coming back, growing their base of support in wider sections of the community.

One of the most passionate members of their Community Bill of Rights Committee is a black woman named Hattie Wilkins, who serves with the Mahoning Valley Organizing Collaborative (MVOC) doing voter registration. Wilkins worked as a union shop steward and is active in promoting local urban gardens so children in her neighborhood can grow up healthy and know where their food comes from. She ran for a Board of

Education position because she is disturbed by the business model that has taken over the local school district. In each of her areas of concern, the Bill of Rights resonated deeply as a real solution to the lack of local control.

HATTIE WILKINS: This is our movement, this is our time. As long as I have breath in my body I'm going to continue to fight for the right to have clean air and clean water and an environment free of human-caused earthquakes, so that's why I will continue to fight for this Community Bill of Rights, not just for myself but for my grandkids and great grandkids as well as for my community.

In 2015, the industry spent over $400,000 against them, in spite of which they came so close that they even paid for their own recount. November 2016 is their sixth time on the ballot and at the time of writing they've already gathered nearly twice the amount of signatures needed. The persistence of the Youngstown group serves as inspiration for other Ohio communities.

SUSIE BEIERSDORFER: I ask people: "What legacy are we leaving our children?" Before, in 2011, when I engaged with people, I was being a neutral scientist, with a list of the frack waste chemicals in hand, but I can't be neutral anymore. If we can't create a sustainable community at the local level, then we can't take care of our own.

As in Colorado, Organizers Bring a Class Action Lawsuit

In 2014, Bass Energy and Ohio Valley Energy got a permit to drill a new well and sued Broadview Heights. O'Dell took to her city council a letter from CELDF offering to defend the city, which was promptly rejected. The council preferred that their own city attorney perform that job, but this fellow chose not to defend the amendment on a rights basis, but rather on a home rule defense—an approach MADION and CELDF knew was bound to fail. At that point O'Dell and MADION tried to intervene to become a defendant representing residents in the lawsuit, but they were denied. So, just as had happened in Colorado, in December 2014 the group, supported by CELDF but working in conjunction with local attorneys Terry Lodge and James Kinsman, filed a class action lawsuit against the state, the drillers, and the Oil and Gas Association. Tish O'Dell and two other Broadview Heights residents stepped up as plaintiffs.

The judge in the first case ruled against the city, declaring drillers have the right to drill because the state permitted the activity. The judge in the class action suit ruled against the residents, not even allowing oral arguments. MADION filed an appeal. In January 2016, they managed to at least enter the courtroom where their attorney, Terry Lodge, got ten minutes to present the case. On the state's side ten lawyers defended the drillers and the state's case, and in March 2016 the Ohio Court rejected the appeal, affirming corporate rights and state preemption of Broadview Heights residents' rights and the right to self-govern. MADION then filed a motion

The Right to Self-Government
If you can't exercise it where you live, you can't exercise it anywhere

Broadview Heights Community Bill of Rights Law passed 2012 with 67% of the vote

to reconsider their decision to respond to the one small breakthrough in one of the judge's rulings in appeals court. In her opinion she recognized that the incorporated municipality is not the same as "the people." This is the first time a court recognized this distinction—recognized in effect that residents may have their own rights separate from the municipal corporation—but the rest of the ruling ignored this point. As O'Dell said: "that judge opened the door but refused to step through." Even though chances are the court won't reconsider, it's important to get the arguments into the public record where other interested parties can see them and be educated.

When at first it was difficult to find plaintiffs for the lawsuit, to get people to sign on, Tish O'Dell didn't hesitate. Just as she didn't hesitate when earlier CELDF invited her to come on board as their official Ohio organizer. A passionate advocate, she quit her day job, giving up retirement benefits, in order to work with CELDF and try to "save the planet for her son." She is kept busy traveling around the state and taking on the next challenges, as the city of Columbus is kicking off their Community Bill of Rights petition campaign and five counties—Medina, Athens, Meigs, Franklin, and Portage—are working to place county home rule charters on their ballot.

County Home Rule Charters

In Ohio there are eighty-eight counties and only two have home rule charters. People who live in the other eighty-six counties can't do any kind of lawmaking without the state's permission. As we have seen, residents of home rule municipalities enjoy at least some self-governing rights that include initiative, referendum, and recall alongside an ability to amend their local governmental charters and the right to enact local laws through their elected representatives. But much too often these local representatives act as administrators of state law. And while the initiative process provides a remedy, county and State functionaries often discourage the people from voting on citizen-initiated legislation. So in the effort to guarantee the right to local self-government, county residents are proposing the first ever county home rule charters with bill of right protections by initiative in the state.

In the last election cycle five counties tried to adopt similar home rule charters. These counties collected their signatures for a total of nine thousand signatures, but when these were turned into their county board of elections, in four counties twelve residents filed protests with each of those boards of elections against the county charters. Not surprisingly, the law firm that represented these twelve home rule objectors represents oil and gas interests. Also not surprisingly, the secretary of state sided with them. In his letter to object to the county petitions being placed on the ballot, he declared that he was "unmoved by the people's argument" and had the "unfettered authority to decide if initiatives by the people were unconstitutional." Fortunately, the state supreme court did not agree with this imperious statement.

Just as had happened in Colorado, community rights activist residents of the counties filed a lawsuit to the Ohio Supreme Court suing Secretary of State John Husted. As in Colorado, the Ohio Supreme Court ruled that only after people vote for a ballot initiative can someone then challenge the constitutionality of the passed law by taking it to the court for a ruling. Husted had also made the argument that because the charters prohibited some activities associated with oil and gas drilling, they were illegal. The court overruled him on this argument as well. Even though the supreme court ruled in the people's favor, they did manage to keep the initiatives off the ballot during the next election cycle for procedural reasons. Not deterred by the court's decision, but rather empowered by it, residents of Athens, Medina, Portage, and Meirs Counties started circulating petitions to get their revamped charters with their county bills of rights onto the November 2016 ballot.

As rights-based organizing expanded to more municipalities and counties in Ohio, in 2013 twenty-five organizers from all over the state came together to form the Ohio Community Rights Network (OHCRN). They currently have thirteen counties represented and participating. At the gathering they signed the Columbus Declaration, with the eventual goal of driving community rights into the state constitution by means of a people initiated constitutional amendment, thereby ending preemption of local law by the state once and for all.

Organizing Issues

As word spreads of this new approach to taking back power at the local level, the Ohio organizers are dealing with lots of issues: How to address people's ignorance or denial about how our current structure of government operates, genuine fears about jobs, finding funding to compete with well-funded opposition, how to engage those not in the choir, and how to find common ground with other groups and build coalitions.

Shale gas has been effectively sold as a solution for both energy and job needs, in part because of the deep history of oil drilling in the state (John D. Rockefeller founded the Standard Oil Company in Cleveland). Other manufacturing like steel has resulted in a mentality welcoming to the next industry that will bring back the wealth. There's a strong belief, unfounded in reality, that the gas industry not only provides a clean form of energy but also a major source of employment. Members of OHCRN have researched the jobs brought in by the gas industry and found their numbers way over inflated.

SUSIE BEIERSDORFER: It's all we hear—jobs, jobs, jobs. And the local newspaper doesn't support our ballot initiative on the basis of jobs. But when I ask the people I meet, can you name me one person who has gotten a job, they can't.

People were told that the Vallourec Company, which makes the steel pipes needed for the pipeline construction, would bring 350 local job plus temporary construction jobs. When the group started to do research, they found out that 85 workers had already been laid off and 170 people went to part-time work. Of course this is a complex issue because no one wants to put anyone else out of work. In a saner system, pipefitters could find jobs in the renewable energy sector.

Protest in Ohio.

HATTIE WILKINS: Yes, we want jobs, but we also want jobs that are safe. We don't want to work a job for six months and to take fifty years to undo the harm that the job did to us, so that's why I am fighting for this Community Bill of Rights.

Ohio is deeply rooted in union labor, and the community rights movement needs to align with workers' rights as it has been able to do in Spokane, and in Colorado. For all too long the environmental movement and the labor movement have been at odds, a rift that corporations have used to increase their profits and power. That is beginning to change as the climate crisis has demonstrated that the issues of labor and environment cannot be addressed separately. The same system that exploits labor and destroys the environment treats some places and people as disposable. To solve all these interrelated problems presents an unprecedented opportunity to find common ground and work together. But it's not easy for people to let go of their belief in separation.

Tɪsʜ O'Dᴇʟʟ: When we talk about pipelines, the regulatory agency allows people to propose a different route, but it can't be about just getting your own community out of harm's way. People still seem to believe they can separate from nature and that they can make money from drilling on their own property as if air and water stay within property boundaries. It's not easy to puncture this denial, and I'm more blunt than I used to be. I say: "Are you willing to let your kids breathe those toxic chemicals from those wells in your neighborhood? Buying organic won't save you."

Finding Allies

For organizers there is always a balancing act between finding common ground with other groups and keeping it real, but coalition-building holds great potential for empowering a movement. In Youngstown they have thirty people actively working together in the FrackFree Mahoning Valley group, not all of them only on community rights. They have been able to find common ground with the approximately three hundred citizens concerned about Mill Creek Park who are now trying to remove the executive director. As in Spokane, as in Colorado and Oregon, community rights work has tremendous potential for bringing together people with different concerns as they begin to recognize they are all trying to wrest power from a rigged system. Groups supporting each other's mission include: Friends of the Mahoning River; TreezPlease, a nonprofit that connects children and nature; the First Unitarian Church of Youngstown, which hosts the group's weekly meeting; and the majority-black Mount Hope Veterans Memorial Park Cemetery group, the latter in response to deep drilling rights having been sold under the cemetery space.

Finding allies among the more traditional or established environmental organizations is much more difficult. If they have not proven themselves aligned to the rights-based approach that CELDF advocates, it can call into question some of their assumptions and accomplishments, as well as their position of expertise and privilege. And, for the same reason, environmental and other lawyers, embedded as they are within settled law, often line up against CELDF's work.

Building coalitions with marginalized communities holds great promise, as expanding community rights work into more urban areas has increased the presence of diversity within organizing ranks. Communities of color should be natural allies, as these communities have been long accustomed to their homes being located within sacrifice zones, from the placing of incinerators and refineries—with resulting spikes in asthma and other illnesses, to the highways slicing through their commercial districts and residential neighborhoods.

However, in some places in Ohio black ministers and preachers have spoken out on the side of the gas industry as a source of jobs. The gas industry had a strategy from the start. They sent their land men to the churches and the schools to advocate signing leases to drill. Now lots of churches have wells on their grounds. And their congregants believe that surely the school wouldn't have let drilling occur next to playgrounds if it weren't safe. They believe the church would not have allowed it. The land men kept coming to the neighborhoods to get more leases signed. Once it starts to dawn that fracking is harmful to the health and safety of residents, much of the community is already under lease. OHCRN organizers can provide a remedy by educating residents, and introducing them to community rights work, hopefully stopping more lease contracts from being signed.

Youngstown is a case in point. Over their four plus years of working together, FrackFree Mahoning Valley has become much more diverse. Another of their most outspoken members is the Reverend Young Tensley, a minister from the Mount Gilead Baptist Church, who has been active in trying to protect Mill Creek Park from fracking. Tensley is a passionate advocate of public water protection and supporter of community rights. During the last election cycle, this minister preached participation from the pulpit and read radio spots for the ballot initiative. The Youngstown organizers consider themselves fortunate to have the opportunity to build bridges across the racial divide.

TISH O'DELL: In some of our community rights workshops we're getting attendees from Black Lives Matter and the United Auto Workers union. It's exciting to introduce them to the idea that with this approach, it's not about begging the police to think first before they shoot young black men. It's not about begging corporations to give nonunion workers the same rights that union workers have. It's about making municipal laws about policing and public policy. When that clicks in, it opens up radical new possibilities.

Chapter 7

The Call: Building a New U.S. Constitution and Advancing Rights Abroad

State CRNs Move toward Amending State Constitutions

Approximately half a million people are now living under the new laws and frameworks described in this book. Communities in other states, such as Maine, New York, New Mexico, Maryland, and Virginia, have also passed ordinances into law, and in yet other places people are taking up the struggle to do so. Instead of spending their energy on begging the structures of power for relief and rights, they are instead working to create the kinds of communities they want to live in, governed by a law they can live by and support. As these ordinances directly challenge the legal authority of corporations and the state to override community decision making, they are a powerful tool for spreading the broader critical movement for the rights of both human and natural communities.

Making sustainability legal means not only people asserting their local democratic power to bring into being economic alternatives such as co-ops, mutual aid networks, community-owned renewable energy, and other projects. The community rights movement also seeks to broaden its coalition to align with the movement for workers' rights, such as the campaign for a decent minimum wage, paid family leave, etc., by mandating those changes in municipal communities. The movement toward a saner and fairer economic system needs the community rights movement because dismantling the system of corporate/governmental power is essential to the evolution and growth of economic alternatives.

Changing settled law in this way is not a short-term project. As citizens turn to the courts to change settled law, they start to recognize that this process may take many, many years. Organizers on the ground, side by side with CELDF, are therefore engaged in examining what other mechanisms will get communities what they want—a right to self-governance driven into the framework of law. Home rule charters are one such mechanism. State-based Community Rights Networks are another way to foster long-term resilience and movement-building.

KENNY AUSUBEL: Nature's favorite forms of organization are networks, and the network's primary function is communication.

Pennsylvania was first, when the Pennsylvania Community Rights Network (PACRN) launched in February 2010. About forty group members from thirteen counties gathered together in Chambersburg, and pledged to work together to "expand civil and political rights for individuals and communities, recognize the rights of nature, and elevate those rights above the 'rights' currently claimed by corporations and other business entities." They issued the Chambersburg Declaration, a document that evolved naturally from the many local ordinances adopted by Pennsylvania township governments. Many elected officials had also signed resolutions asking for a Pennsylvania Constitutional Convention. The declaration asserts that communities in Pennsylvania—because they are deprived of decision-making power by state legislation and live under a constitutional structure that favors corporate rights—have the responsibility to call for a new state constitutional structure.

From the Chambersburg Declaration:

That a Call Issues from this Gathering:

To create a network of people committed to securing the right to local, community self-government, the reversal of political, legal, and cultural doctrines that interfere with that right, and the creation of a new system and doctrines that support that right;

To call upon the people and elected officials across the Commonwealth of Pennsylvania to convene a larger gathering of delegates representing their municipal communities, who will propose constitutional changes to secure the right of local, community self-government; and

To create the people's movement that will result in these changes to the Pennsylvania Constitution.

CELDF organizers Ben Price and Chad Nicholson worked closely with PACRN members as their work evolved. Eventually thirteen board members were elected. They proceeded to hold monthly conference calls and define for themselves how to further their mission. The network provides resources for communities wanting to assert their rights via ordinance, community rights workshops, copies of the various ordinances that might be used, and a speakers' bureau. The group proceeded to work closely with Price and Nicholson to draft the language of a state constitutional amendment.

In Pennsylvania, to amend the state constitution, the initiative must first be introduced by a member of the house or senate, after which both houses of the legislature must vote to pass the initiative, two years in a row. Then the proposed amendment goes on the ballot and must be passed by a two-thirds majority. The problem with introducing the amendment via the legislature is that recognizing a right to local self-government would likely never leave committee because it challenges the very power of the legislators involved. This is such an impossibly onerous process that PACRN decided that a better strategy might be to work to pass an amendment to change how the constitution is amended so that the people themselves can initiate the change. Such a change could be proposed as an increase in democracy, following the example of other states, giving the people more of a voice. They might be able to embarrass the political powers into such a move.

They might hark back to the first version of the Pennsylvania constitution, which was a lot more flexible. In 1776 the people had all the control, when Pennsylvania's was maybe the most democratic constitution in the young states. How its principles were changed and altered over time during different eras is something that can be learned through the Democracy School's more state-specific curriculum, now taught as a one-day community rights workshop. Here the legal concepts that deprive residents of rights are deconstructed, and the amendment process is explored.

Colorado Constitutional Amendment Moves to the Ballot

States have different systems of amending their constitutions. In Colorado the amendment can be placed directly onto the state ballot by residents of the state. The Colorado Community Rights Network (COCRN) is strong and actively pursuing an amendment to the state constitution which would carve out expanded municipal authority for communities to adopt rights-based laws. After a final approval by the Colorado Supreme Court in March 2016, and if the network collects enough signatures to qualify the amendment, the Community Rights Amendment will be voted on for the first time in the U.S. in the November 2016 election. (See Chapter 5.)

State of Ohio Tries to Co-opt the Call

Organizers on the ground in Ohio formed the Ohio Community Rights Network (OHCRN) in 2013. With thirteen counties represented and participating, they started out strong with their Columbus Declaration, similar to the Chambersburg Declaration. (See pp. 117–19.) The OHCRN serves a few different functions. They assist local communities who are active in passing community rights ordinances. They provide resources to Ohio communities who are working on a bill of rights, literature and well-designed flyers, and copies of the initiatives themselves so that folks in each new community don't have to reinvent the wheel. As has happened in Pennsylvania, they have also developed a one-day specific Ohio community rights workshop which they bring to communities all over the state, sometimes as often as twice a month, and have nearly completed work on an organizer handbook.

The OHCRN has drafted language for a state constitutional amendment and is exploring how to start the campaign in the best possible way. Passing an amendment to the state constitution by initiative petition is a strenuous process. After the initial signature gathering phase, the attorney general has to approve the language, a process that takes time and has its own pitfalls, and only then can it move to the ballot but not before they have gathered over six hundred thousand signatures to qualify the initiative for the ballot.

At the beginning of this campaign to launch the ballot initiative, OHCRN members are discussing what strategy to employ to yield the biggest impact. Timing is up for debate. What kind of events can create the most buzz as well as the depth of understanding required to pass such a bill? Members are beginning to use video and a play entitled *The People vs. the Corporate State* as innovative means of spreading the message.

Gathering that many signatures and doing the accompanying education is an especially daunting task as many OHCRN members are also busy getting their new county charters finalized and collecting signatures to qualify for the county ballots. But organizers remind themselves, as Nelson Mandela famously said: It always seems impossible until it's done.

TISH O'DELL: I spend a lot of my time educating and hopefully inspiring people to do something. People get depressed. The network is great because everyone has up and down days, and some people feel bad when they get down, so we can rely on each other for mutual support and to be reminded that we *are* making a difference. Community means we're there to help each other get back up.

Tish O'Dell from Ohio.

The State of Ohio has responded to this potential demand for constitutional change by trying to co-opt the call. Every twenty years a question appears on the ballot asking if there should be an Ohio Constitutional Convention, to determine whether the state's constitution is meeting the needs of the people or whether it needs amending. Over the past several decades, people have voted against holding such a convention. In 2012, Governor Kasich determined that instead of holding such a convention, he would appoint a commission to study the need for constitutional change. It's not surprising that the thirty-two appointed commission members are all from the industrial, legal, and entrenched governance sector, mostly current and retired politicians, judges, corporate lawyers, and academics. Even more offensive, one member supposedly representing the public is a corporate lawyer also representing the Nexus pipeline—a proposed natural gas pipeline slated for construction through Ohio. It's a sure bet that any changes the commission proposes will only make the constitution even friendlier to industry. The good news is that community rights organizers in Ohio are not fooled.

New Hampshire's Constitutional Amendment Gets a Sponsor in the Legislature

In New Hampshire, any attempt to amend the state's constitution must first gain 60 percent support of the state government, in both houses of that government, to be placed on the ballot for a general election. So after the New Hampshire Community Rights Network crafted the language for their constitutional amendment, they started working on finding someone in the legislature to sponsor the bill.

Chris Mills, chair of the legislative committee of the NHCRN, and Michelle Sanborn took on the task of finding the legislators. Most in the legislature had never heard of community rights, and this created the need for all sorts of educational conversations. Because of the democratic structure of the town meeting and selectmen who must answer to those they represent locally, people tend to think democratic power is alive and well in the state and can ignore the fact that the town boards have little actual authority.

In 2015, NHCRN tried but failed to find a sponsor for the bill, but in early 2016, they gave a presentation in Rindge, in Cheshire County and the state representative for that district attended. Representative Susan Emerson learned all about the proposed amendment and proceeded to sign on as an enthusiastic prime sponsor of the bill. Once Emerson submitted the paperwork, other representatives were willing to sign on and the bill gained three Democrats and two Republicans as cosponsors.

MICHELLE SANBORN: The bipartisan split is good, as it reveals that the community rights issue reaches way beyond the blue/red divide. Community Rights work does however reveal other divides: Those in poor areas under direct threat versus those from more populated areas not under direct threat, who want industry and the money that may bring.

NHCRN spoke at a public hearing on community rights at the House Legislative Administration Committee in Concord. In New Hampshire, by law, every bill that is presented must have a public hearing. That doesn't mean there is discourse, or that anyone has to listen. The House Legislative Administrative Committee voted unanimously to recommend to the house to kill the bill and then placed it on the consent calendar. This means that instead of moving onto the floor to be discussed it's bundled with a bunch of other legislative matters. The house then voted out forty-six issues of legislation in fifteen minutes and that was the end of the Community Rights Amendment for this session.

The NHCRN will bring back the bill again in 2017, and in the meantime keep working to educate other legislators and lay folks. To gain more cosponsors and support, they intend to present community rights workshops over the summer, especially focusing on the more populated communities in the southern parts of the state threatened by pipelines.

MICHELLE SANBORN: Our work is a marathon, not a sprint.

National Community Rights Network: Amending the U.S. Constitution

To provide mutual support in this marathon, and to grow the movement, members from the various state community rights networks decided to form a national organization as well. The first meeting of the National Community Rights Network (NCRN) took place April 8, 2015, in Youngstown, Ohio. Seven states were represented. The group chose as their board of directors two members from each state's Community Rights Network. They aim to build from the bottom up to expand the work. All who were present at the gathering were active organizers in their states and possessed a direct, experiential understanding of the issues and problems encountered in local community rights work.

As CELDF's national organizing director, Ben Price served as the liaison between NCRN and CELDF. The relationship of CELDF to the National Community Rights Network mirrors its relationship to the state networks. As the organization that supported the thinking and gave structure to the lawmaking in the communities, CELDF functions as a sort of midwife to the movement for community rights, but it is not "leading the charge." Nor, as a small nonprofit with its hands overfull, can it do so. The networks are self-evolving, with CELDF's guidance.

BEN PRICE: I don't sit on the board, but I join in on the conference calls and chime in on occasion. CELDF's role is to make sure that discussion and mutual support are outcome driven and foster engagement in projects that educate people to move toward constitutional change at state level.

In October 2015, they convened their first gathering independent of CELDF. The members began the meeting with discussing and declaring their purpose. Named after two much-beloved activists who had helped form their state Community Rights Networks and who had died that year, members from seven states signed the "Darrell-Moore declaration," which on a national level resembles the declarations from the states with its main long-term purpose of constitutional change on the federal level. The process of crafting the document helped members clarify the mission of this fledging organization.

To start the campaign of going for a federal constitutional amendment, they worked with a CELDF legal team to draft language that is now available on their website. A committee wrote a proposed Twenty-Eighth Amendment to the U.S. Constitution, which would recognize a federally protected right of local community self-government. More immediate goals are to build the network itself, to strengthen ties between existing state networks, and to support and endorse the various state-based efforts (including, for instance, the New Hampshire CRN's first appearance in the legislature).

Currently, Ohio activist Susie Beiersdorfer chairs the NCRN board. As the organizer who also is a driver of the Youngstown campaign, now on its sixth attempt to pass their Bill of Rights, which would ban fracking within the city, this is a woman who embodies persistence. Knowing that the effort to change the constitution is, in her words, a long way down the road, she also knows it's important for the group to foster long-term resilience, which includes focusing on the right things.

Ohio Supreme Court Says Towns Aren't Allowed To Ban Fracking

BY BILLY CORRIHER - GUEST CONTRIBUTOR & SEAN WRIGHT - GUEST CONTRIBUTOR FEB 19, 2015 9:21AM

In this May 27. 2011 Photo T.J. Turner stands in Yellow Springs, Ohio, near a sign protesting the practice of fracking, a process used to extract oil or natural gas from hard rock formations.

As communities have begun to assert their rights, corporations and the courts have responded by filing lawsuits and further limiting the people's lawmaking authority.

SUSIE BEIERSDORFER: A win at the polls isn't necessarily a win if people don't stand behind it. People get excited about getting a particular candidate in, but that doesn't begin to deal with the systemic change we need. So it's necessary to redefine what a win is. Getting defeated by only two hundred votes in Youngstown, that was a huge win, considering all the money that was spent against us.

Of course the NCRN is a fledging organization, and its members' energy is mostly being spent locally. To progress to the federal effort, members of the NCRN know they need more states involved, and that means increasing their capacity, their man- and woman-power. While there are plenty of new folks who are calling for help, and who want to get involved, it's going to take a much larger cadre of well-trained organizers to respond to the needs on the ground, build the movement, and to spread the word. To that end, Ben Price has drafted an organizers' guide, and the NCRN is now offering a speakers' bureau training program. What is most needed to have a movement is people, and speaking tours are part of the strategy.

Dr. Tom Groover, one of the two NCRN members from Colorado, advocated that the first order of business be communication between the CRN's and the creation of a committee to foster that communication. Not just to determine how best to communicate with each other, but how to get the word out to those not already participating. He is concerned with the need to be media savvy and to have a communications strategy. There isn't much out there about community rights in alternative media, let alone the corporate mainstream media. Groover has been conducting interviews on video with some of the community rights organizers so they can tell their stories and express their ideas in depth, making them available on a YouTube channel.

Dr. Tom Groover: We need to bring out our case to the public in defense of the right of self-government. And we also need to define our terms, because there's little comprehension out there. When you say "community rights," a lot of people draw a blank. Who knows what a community is anymore? Many of us have a mall instead. And the idea of rights, where do they come from, and what is the difference between legal rights, inalienable rights, and natural rights? Unless we define our terms, folks won't know what we want to defend.

This is in part the challenge of a movement in which most people get involved to fight against something, before they slowly begin to define what they are fighting for. As the community rights movement reaches toward greater visibility, it will lead with its vision, the translation of community rights and rights for nature into law. This lawmaking includes civil disobedience, which is a powerful aspect of movement-building that is sure to grow in the future.

Civil disobedience is one way to draw attention to and clarify the ideas and make them visible and understood in the broader culture. Ultimately the solutions may not to be found in the courts, which are part of the system and set up to keep the people out. The task is to go beyond the legal system and to build solidarity and coalitions willing to work for fundamental change. And this begins by educating and inspiring people to claim their own fundamental rights as well as nature's right to exist, flourish, and evolve.

The Rights of Nature Gain Traction Abroad

Tamaqua Borough was the first community to legally recognize nature's right to exist. Since that time, other communities in Pennsylvania, New Hampshire, New York, Maryland, Ohio, New Mexico, Colorado, and other states have adopted new laws that change the status of natural communities and ecosystems from being regarded as property under the law to being recognized as rights-bearing entities. These laws recognize that natural communities and ecosystems possess a fundamental right to exist and flourish and that residents possess the legal authority to enforce those rights on behalf of the ecosystem.

Ecuador's New Constitution

In 2007 an international nonprofit organization that supports indigenous people in the Amazon in claiming stewardship over local rainforests learned of CELDF's work and asked for assistance. The driving concern of the Pachamama Alliance was to give the indigenous people of Ecuador the rights that have been denied to native tribes throughout the Americas, rights that would in turn empower the tribes to protect their natural environment and rainforests. It turned out that the country was engaged in a rewrite of its constitution and rethinking some fundamental principles.

In Montecristi, a town on the Ecuadorian coast, Linzey and CELDF associate Mari Margil presented rights-of-nature concepts to committees within Ecuador's Constituent Assembly tasked with drafting the new constitution. They also met with the president of the assembly, Alberto Acosta. CELDF was asked to draft provisions on the rights of nature for assembly members. That spring and summer, the assembly voted to adopt these fundamental rights, and in September 2008 the new constitution was approved by an overwhelming margin through a national referendum vote. With that vote, Ecuador became the first country in the world to codify a new system of environmental protection based on the rights of nature—an exceptional event that gives hope to people struggling all over the world.

Since that time, increasing numbers of communities, organizations, and governments around the world are seeking a new path to protect nature. CELDF has engaged with groups in Ghana, Cameroon, Kenya, Canada, Spain, the United Kingdom, the European Union, and elsewhere on advancing rights-of-nature legal frameworks.

In 2010 Ecuador's neighbor, Bolivia, held the World People's Conference on Climate Change and the Rights of Mother Earth. During this conference CELDF helped draft the Universal Declaration on the Rights of Mother Earth. Modeled on the UN Universal Declaration of Human Rights, adopted in 1948, this document holds that the rights of

Mother Earth are inalienable and inherent, and that the "rights of each being are limited by the rights of other beings and any conflict between their rights must be resolved in a way that maintains the integrity, balance and health of Mother Earth." After the conference, Bolivia submitted this beautifully worded and groundbreaking declaration to the UN General Assembly but no action has yet been forthcoming from UN.

In that same year, at a meeting held in Tamate, Ecuador, the Global Alliance for the Rights of Nature was formed with founding members from Africa, Australia, and North and South America, united in their purpose of building an international rights of nature movement.

The following year, Ecuador's Rights of Nature constitutional provisions were tested in the courts for the first time. The Provincial Court of Justice of Loha heard a case in which the Vilcabamba River was a plaintiff seeking to defend its constitutional rights against a government highway project. Even though the court upheld the new provisions and ruled against the project, this positive action did not stop the project. Because of this, in 2012, when Bolivia adopted its Law under the Mother Earth and Integral Development for Living Well, both civil society and indigenous peoples in Bolivia, much like in Ecuador, questioned whether the new law would in fact uphold the rights of ecosystems. Both Bolivia and Ecuador's presidents seek to appear "green" even as they propose major development and mining projects that will severely compromise and damage their countries' ecosystems.

At the same time in 2012, with the Himalayan glaciers melting due to global warming and developing nations such as Nepal seeing little progress through the UN climate change negotiations, CELDF developed a Right to Climate legal framework in a draft for Rights of Nature constitutional provisions to the Nepal Constituent Assembly. Under this framework the atmosphere, as well as human and natural communities, have the right to a healthy, functioning climate free from human alteration, which is a hugely exciting development. This would create a legal platform whereby at-risk countries could hold major polluters around the world responsible for their global warming impacts.

CELDF also began working in India on a national legislative campaign to recognize rights for the Ganga River Basin; an ecosystem depended upon by half a billion people. Yet the river and its tributaries are facing severe degradation due to pollution, water withdrawals, and other practices. CELDF is partnering with Ganga Action Paravar and the Global Interfaith WASH Alliance-India in this work.

As well in 2012, while not directly CELDF-related, in a widening use of the rights-of-nature concept, the government of New Zealand reached agreement with the Whanganui River iwi, a local Maori people, to recognize a legal persona, in a form of legal standing, for the Whanganui River. This development meant that, moving forward, the government and the iwi people would share guardianship of the river and determine appropriate protection measures.

In 2013, CELDF participated in Australia's Earth Laws Alliance's Wild Law Conference, and a speaking tour, advocating community rights and rights of nature. In Spain and Australia, CELDF has helped NGO partners to develop Community Bill of Rights laws for communities, each containing the rights of nature, addressing corporate rights, and prohibiting certain corporate activities.

CELDF also began working with the indigenous Raizal people of the San Andrés Archipelago of Colombia, to advance community rights and the rights of nature on the islands. CELDF presented at the annual Raizal Emancipation Week in 2015, and began working with them to develop their own version of the Democracy School with a curriculum based on their own history of colonization and oppression. CELDF will be drafting a Raizal Bill of Rights with them to establish their rights to self-governance and the rights of nature.

That the rights-of-nature concept is gaining in popularity can be witnessed by Pope Francis's September 2015 address to the United Nations. He stated that a true "right of the environment" does exist. And in his encyclical on climate change he calls for "The establishment of a legal framework which can set clear boundaries and ensure the protection of ecosystems."

In 2016, CELDF worked with members of the Green Party of England and Wales to draft and adopt a rights of nature policy platform.

In late 2015, CELDF began working the Ho-Chunk Nation, which in September took the first steps to codify the rights of nature in its constitution. If they persist in their effort, they would become the first tribe in the U.S. to do so.

Once people are introduced to the concept of basing law in the scientific reality of nature as a living interactive entity in which we are all embedded, instead of dead matter to buy and sell, it shifts thinking. This is clearly an idea whose time has come. Now the work before us all is to translate this shift in thinking into further action and lawmaking.

Additions to the Ecuador Constitution

Article 1. Nature or Pachamama, where life is reproduced and exists, has the right to exist, persist, maintain itself and regenerate its own vital cycles, structure, functions, and its evolutionary processes.

Any person, people, community, or nationality, may demand the observance of the rights of the natural environment before public bodies. The application and interpretation of these rights will follow the related principles established in the Constitution.

Article 2. Nature has the right to be completely restored. This complete restoration is independent of the obligation on natural and juridical persons or the State to compensate people or collective groups that depend on the natural systems.

In the cases of severe or permanent environmental impact, including the ones caused by the exploitation of nonrenewable natural resources, the State will establish the most efficient mechanisms for the restoration, and will adopt the adequate measures to eliminate or mitigate the harmful environmental consequences.

Article 3. The State will motivate natural and juridical persons as well as collectives to protect nature; it will promote respect towards all the elements that form an ecosystem.

Article 4. The State will apply precaution and restriction measures in all the activities that can lead to the extinction of species, the destruction of the ecosystems, or the permanent alteration of the natural cycles.

The introduction of organisms and organic and inorganic material that can alter in a definitive way the national genetic heritage is prohibited.

Article 5. The persons, people, communities, and nationalities will have the right to benefit from the environment and form natural wealth that will allow well-being.

The Chambersburg Declaration: The Founding Document of the PA Community Rights Network

Signed in Chambersburg, Pennsylvania, on Saturday, February 20, 2010

We declare:

That the political, legal, and economic systems of the United States allow, in each generation, an elite few to impose policy and governing decisions that threaten the very survival of human and natural communities;

That the goal of those decisions is to concentrate wealth and greater governing power through the exploitation of human and natural communities, while promoting the belief that such exploitation is necessary for the common good;

That the survival of our communities depends on replacing this system of governance by the privileged with new community-based democratic decision-making systems;

That environmental and economic sustainability can be achieved only when the people affected by governing decisions are the ones who make them;

That, for the past two centuries, people have been unable to secure economic and environmental sustainability primarily through the existing minority-rule system, laboring under the myth that we live in a democracy;

That most reformers and activists have not focused on replacing the current system of elite decision-making with a democratic one, but have concentrated merely on lobbying the factions in power to make better decisions; and

That reformers and activists have not halted the destruction of our human or natural communities because they have viewed economic and environmental ills as isolated problems, rather than as symptoms produced by the absence of democracy.

Therefore, let it be resolved:

That a people's movement must be created with a goal of revoking the authority of the corporate minority to impose political, legal, and economic systems that endanger our human and natural communities;

That such a movement shall begin in the municipal communities of Pennsylvania;

That we, the people, must transform our individual community struggles into new frameworks of law that dismantle the existing undemocratic systems while codifying new, sustainable systems;

That such a movement must grow and accelerate through the work of people in all municipalities to raise the profile of this work at state and national levels;

That when corporate and governmental decision-makers challenge the people's right to assert local, community self-governance through passage of municipal law, the people, through their municipal governments, must openly and frontally defy those legal and political doctrines that subordinate the rights of the people to the privileges of a few;

That those doctrines include preemption, subordination of municipal governments; bestowal of constitutional rights upon corporations, and relegating ecosystems to the status of property;

That those communities in defiance of rights-denying law must join with other communities in our state and across the nation to envision and build new state and federal constitutional structures that codify new, rights-asserting systems of governance;

That Pennsylvania communities have worked for more than a decade to advance those new systems and, therefore, have the responsibility to become the first communities to call for a new state constitutional structure; and

That now, this 20th day of February, 2010, the undersigned pledge to begin that work, which will drive the right to local, community self-government into the Pennsylvania Constitution, thus liberating Pennsylvania communities from the legal and political doctrines that prevent them from building economically and environmentally sustainable communities.

That a Call Issues from This Gathering:
To create a network of people committed to securing the right to local, community self-government, the reversal of political, legal, and cultural doctrines that interfere with that right, and the creation of a new system and doctrines that support that right;

To call upon the people and elected officials across the Commonwealth of Pennsylvania to convene a larger gathering of delegates representing their municipal communities, who will propose constitutional changes to secure the right of local, community self-government; and

    To create the people's movement that will result in these changes to the Pennsylvania Constitution.

Appendix
Ordinances and Charters

Home Rule Charter of the Township of Grant, Indiana County, Pennsylvania

ARTICLE I – BILL OF RIGHTS

Section 101. All legitimate governments in the United States owe their existence to the people of the community that those governments serve, and governments exist to secure and protect the rights of the people and those communities. Any system of government that becomes destructive of those ends is not legitimate, lawful, or constitutional.

Section 102. The people of Grant Township possess both the collective and individual right of self-government in their local community, the right to a system of government that embodies that right, and the right to a system of government that protects and secures their human, civil, and collective rights.

Section 103. The people of Grant Township possess the right to use their local government to make law, and the making and enforcement of law by the people through a municipal corporation, or any other institution, shall not eliminate, limit, or reduce their sovereign right of local community self-government.

Section 104. All residents of Grant Township, along with natural communities and ecosystems within the Township, possess the right to clean air, water, and soil, which shall include the right to be free from activities which may pose potential risks to clean air, water, and soil within the Township, including the depositing of waste from oil and gas extraction.

Section 105. All residents of Grant Township possess the right to the scenic, historic, and aesthetic values of the Township, including unspoiled vistas and a rural quality of life. That right shall include the right of the residents of the Township to be free from activities which threaten scenic, historic, and aesthetic values, including from the depositing of waste from oil and gas extraction.

Section 106. Natural communities and ecosystems within Grant Township, including, but not limited to, rivers, streams, and aquifers, possess the right to exist, flourish, and naturally evolve.

Section 107. All residents of Grant Township possess the right to a sustainable energy future, which includes, but is not limited to, the development, production, and use of energy from renewable and sustainable fuel sources, the right to establish local sustainable energy policies to further secure this right, and the right to be free from energy extraction, production, and use that may adversely impact the rights of human communities, natural communities, or ecosystems. The right to a sustainable energy future shall include the right to be free from activities related to fossil fuel extraction and production, including the depositing of waste from oil and gas extraction.

123

Section 108. All residents of Grant Township possess a right to be fairly taxed, which includes property tax assessments and rates that are commensurate with the needs of the Township and the Township's residents, and the services required to meet those needs. Protection of that right shall require the Board of Township Supervisors to review Indiana County's administration of property taxation for Grant Township residents at least once every three years. If the Board of Supervisors deems the administration of property taxation to be unfair, unjust, or burdensome to the residents of Grant Township, the Board of Supervisors shall have the authority, through the adoption of an Ordinance, to change the administration of property taxation.

Section 109. All residents of Grant Township possess the right to enforce the rights and prohibitions secured by this Charter, which shall include the right of Township residents to intervene in any legal action involving the rights and prohibitions recognized by this Charter.

Section 110. All rights secured by this Charter are inherent, fundamental, and unalienable, and shall be self-executing and enforceable against both private and public actors. Further implementing legislation shall not be required for Grant Township, the residents of Grant Township, or the ecosystems and natural communities protected by this Charter, to enforce all of the provisions of this Charter. The rights secured by this Charter shall only be enforceable against actions specifically prohibited by this Charter, unless otherwise specifically noted.

ARTICLE II – GENERAL POWERS OF THE MUNICIPALITY

Section 201. *Status and Title.* The name of the municipality created by this Home Rule Charter shall be "Grant Township" and it shall operate as a Home Rule municipality, and possess the powers and authority of a Home Rule municipality.

Section 202. *Boundaries.* The boundaries of the Township shall be the actual boundaries of the Township at the time this Charter takes effect and as they may be lawfully changed thereafter.

Section 203. *Governing Body.* The governing body of the municipal Home Rule corporation shall be the Board of Supervisors, acting under the authority of, and with the consent of, the people of Grant Township.

Section 204. *Rules of Operation.* Unless expanded or altered as provided by this Charter, the rules of operation for the Grant Township Home Rule municipal corporation shall be the ones provided to second class Townships pursuant to the Second Class Township Code of the Commonwealth of Pennsylvania.

Section 205. *Repeals.* The Articles, sections, policies, and provisions of this Charter hereby repeal the provisions of any prior Ordinances, laws, or rules of the Township that are inconsistent with this Charter.

Section 206. *Legal Claims and Liabilities of the Township.* Upon enactment of this Charter, the Township shall continue to own, possess, and control all legal claims, power, and property of every kind and nature, owned, possessed, or controlled by it prior to when this Charter takes effect, and shall be subject to all its debts, obligations, liabilities, and duties.

Section 207. *Pending Actions and Proceedings.* No enforcement action or proceeding, civil or criminal, which was brought by the Township or any office, department, agency, or officer thereof, pending at the time this Charter takes effect, shall be affected by the adoption of this Charter or by anything herein contained. Any action or proceeding, civil or criminal, filed against the Township or any office, department, agency, or officer thereof, pending at the time this Charter takes effect, shall be evaluated by appropriate legal counsel and, if the transformation to a Home Rule municipality is deemed to transform the nature and character of the proceeding, the Township Board of Supervisors shall instruct legal counsel to request a dismissal of those proceedings.

Section 208. *Continuation of Ordinances.* All Ordinances, resolutions, rules, and regulations, or portions thereof in force when this Charter takes effect, which have been directly incorporated into this Charter, shall be deemed to have been repealed or amended to the extent that they duplicate provisions of this Charter. Other Ordinances, resolutions, rules, and regulations, or portions thereof in force when this Charter takes effect, shall temporarily be continued in force and effect until the Board of Supervisors has reviewed them, and determined to re-adopt them as Ordinances of the Home Rule municipality, or determined that they should be repealed or amended.

Section 209. *Authority of Existing Officers.* The Supervisors in office at the time this Charter takes effect shall remain in office for the full terms for which they were originally elected, and shall receive the same compensation until their terms expire. However, they shall have the responsibilities, duties, and authority only as set forth in and pursuant to this Charter. All other elected officials of the Township in office at the time this Charter takes effect shall remain in office for the full term for which they were elected, and shall receive the same compensation which they received prior to the adoption of this Charter.

ARTICLE III – PROHIBITIONS AND ENFORCEMENT

Section 301. *Depositing of Waste from Oil and Gas Extraction.* It shall be unlawful within Grant Township for any corporation or government to engage in the depositing of waste from oil and gas extraction.

Section 302. *State and Federal Authority.* No permit, license, privilege, charter, or other authorization issued to a corporation, by any State or federal entity, that would violate the prohibitions of this Charter or any rights secured by this Charter, shall be deemed valid within Grant Township.

Section 303. *Summary Offenses.* Any corporation or government that violates any provision of this Charter shall be guilty of an offense and, upon conviction thereof, shall be sentenced to pay the maximum fine allowable under State law for that violation. Each day or portion thereof, and each violation of a section of this Charter, shall count as a separate violation.

Section 304. *Standing for Township and Residents.* Grant Township, or any resident of Grant Township, may enforce the rights and prohibitions of the Charter through an action brought in any court possessing jurisdiction over activities occurring within Grant Township. In such an action, Grant Township or the resident shall be entitled to recover all costs of litigation, including, without limitation, expert and attorney's fees.

Section 305. *Enforcement of Natural Community and Ecosystem Rights.* Ecosystems and natural communities within Grant Township may enforce their rights, and this Charter's prohibitions, through an action brought by Grant Township or residents of Grant Township in the name of the ecosystem or natural community as the real party in interest. Actions may be brought in any court possessing jurisdiction over activities occurring within Grant Township.. Damages shall be measured by the cost of restoring the ecosystem or natural community to its state before the injury, and shall be paid to Grant Township to be used exclusively for the full and complete restoration of the ecosystem or natural community.

Section 306. *Enforcement of State Laws.* All laws adopted by the legislature of the State of Pennsylvania, and rules adopted by any State agency, shall be the law of Grant Township only to the extent that they do not violate the rights or prohibitions recognized by this Charter.

ARTICLE IV – CORPORATE POWERS

Section 401. *Corporate Privileges.* Corporations that violate this Charter or the laws of the Township, or that seek to violate the Charter or those laws, shall not be deemed to be "persons" to the extent that such treatment would interfere with the rights or prohibitions enumerated by this Charter or those laws, nor shall they possess any other legal rights, powers, privileges, immunities, or duties that would interfere with the rights or prohibitions enumerated by the Charter or those laws, including standing to challenge the Charter or laws, the power to assert State or federal preemptive laws in an attempt to overturn the Charter or laws, or the power to assert that the people of Grant Township lack the authority to adopt this Charter or other Township laws.

ARTICLE V – EMERGENCY TOWN MEETING

Section 501. *Emergency Town Meeting.* In the event of a substantial public emergency affecting the health, safety, and welfare of the residents of Grant Township, or an event or activity that would infringe on the rights of the residents of Grant Township, the electors of the Township may call an Emergency Town Meeting whereby the electors of the Township may adopt a proposed Ordinance. If adopted, that Ordinance shall remain valid until the next available election at which the electors of the Township shall have the opportunity to make the Ordinance permanent by amending the Township's Home Rule Charter with the substance of the Ordinance.

Section 502. *Initiation and Petition Form.* To call an Emergency Town Meeting, a petition must be created by the petition filer. Each petition shall bear the name of the petition filer. The petition filer shall deliver written notice, along with a copy of the proposed Ordinance, to the Township Secretary during the hours that the Township office is officially open, and the Township Secretary shall post a copy of that notice and the proposed Ordinance at the Township Building the same day upon receiving that notice. No signatures may be affixed to the petitions until notice of the petition is posted at the Township Building. Each signature shall be in ink and shall be accompanied by the signer's address, signer's printed name, and the date of signing. Only registered electors who are residents of the Township are eligible to sign the petition. The petition shall contain the full text of the proposed Ordinance if that text can fit on a single page. If the text cannot fit on a single page, then circulators shall have full copies of the proposed Ordinance in their possession for inspection by potential signers, and the petition shall identify the Ordinance by declaring that "The signers below call for an Emergency Town Meeting to be held to consider the adoption of the Ordinance filed with the Secretary of the Township on [date] by [petition filer]." On the back of each page of the petition there shall be an attached affidavit executed by the circulator verifying the authenticity of the signers, and that the signers are registered electors who are residents of the Township to the best of the circulator's knowledge. Only registered electors who are residents within the Township may circulate petitions.

Section 503. *Timeline.* Petition circulators shall have 15 (fifteen) calendar days to collect the required signatures, commencing on the date that the Township Secretary posts the petition. The date that the Township Secretary posts the petition shall be included as 1 (one) of the 15 (fifteen) days that circulators may collect signatures. Petition circulators must gather valid signatures equal to at least 30% (thirty percent) of the number of registered electors within the Township. Petitions bearing the requisite number of signatures must then be filed with the Secretary of the Township during the hours that the Township office is officially open, and the Secretary shall issue a written notice of receipt, and then send the signatures to the Emergency Town Meeting Committee for verification. If the 15 (fifteen) day window for signature gathering expires on a day that the Township office is not officially open, the signatures may be submitted to the Township Secretary on the next day that the Township office is officially open; no signatures shall be gathered on the day(s) that fall between the date that the signature gathering window expires and the next day the Township office is officially open.

Section 504. *Verification and the Emergency Town Meeting Committee.* The Emergency Town Meeting Committee shall verify the accuracy and sufficiency of the petition signatures within 10 (ten) days of the date upon which the petitions are submitted to the Township Secretary, and the Committee shall issue a final determination based on its review. Upon receipt of the petitions from the Secretary, the Chairman of the Board of Supervisors shall schedule and advertise, as a special meeting, a meeting of the Emergency Town Meeting Committee. The Emergency Town Meeting Committee shall consist of the Township Secretary, the Chairman of the Board of Supervisors, the Township Auditor who has served for the longest period of time in the capacity of Auditor within the Township, the petition filer, and the Township Tax Collector. A quorum of the Emergency Town Meeting Committee shall consist of three of those individuals. The number of required signatures shall be calculated using current records from the County Board of Elections; the validity of signatures shall be verified using current records from the County Board of Elections. Disputes over the validity of any individual signature shall be resolved by a majority vote of the Emergency Town Meeting Committee.

Section 505. *Court Review.* The petition filer shall be notified of the final determination of the Emergency Town Meeting Committee within one day of the final determination. The final determination of whether the petition satisfies the requirements for the calling of an Emergency Town Meeting shall be subject to judicial review. An appeal of the final determination of the Emergency Town Meeting Committee shall be filed to the Indiana County Court of Common Pleas, and such appeal must be filed within 10 (ten) days of the final determination of the Emergency Town Meeting Committee. Filing of the appeal shall not prejudice the ability of the original petition filer to create, circulate, and qualify a new petition, following the procedures contained within this Charter.

Section 506. *Emergency Town Meeting Preparation.* If the Emergency Town Meeting Committee determines that the petitions meet the requirements imposed by this Article of the Charter, it shall issue a final determination to that effect, and the Committee must set a date for the Emergency Town Meeting, which must occur no later than 15 (fifteen) days after the Emergency Town Meeting Committee has made its final determination. Notices shall be sent via U.S. Mail to all registered electors who are residents of the Township, informing those electors of the date of the Emergency Town

Meeting. The Notices shall also contain a brief summary of the proposed Ordinance, and also a brief overview of the nature of the Emergency Town Meeting, including informing electors that they will have the opportunity to cast a vote on the proposed Ordinance. The Notices shall be sent out no later than 7 (seven) days before the date of the Emergency Town Meeting. Two advertisements, containing the summary of the proposed Ordinance and the date of the Emergency Town Meeting, shall also be published on 2 (two) consecutive days in a newspaper of general circulation within the Township before the meeting is held.

Section 507. *Running of the Meeting.* The Chairman of the Board of Supervisors shall facilitate the Emergency Town Meeting. All Township electors will be issued a ballot upon arrival at the Emergency Town Meeting. The ballots shall be created and printed by the Emergency Town Meeting Committee. The ballot shall contain the summary of the proposed Ordinance, the question "Shall this Ordinance become law within Grant Township?" and a space for the elector to vote "yes" or "no" on the question. Sufficient copies of the full text of the Ordinance shall be available for inspection at the Emergency Town Meeting. The Chairman of the Board of Supervisors shall call the meeting to order. The petition filer shall have ten minutes to present the proposed Ordinance. Public comment shall follow, with registered Township electors having three minutes each to speak. Following public comment, electors shall individually deliver their ballots to the Chairman of the Board of Supervisors; and the Chairman, upon receiving each ballot, shall direct the Township Secretary to verify the name of the elector on records obtained from the County Board of Elections. Once verified, the Chairman shall place the ballot into a container overseen by the Emergency Town Meeting Committee.

Section 508. *Ballot Counting.* When all the votes have been cast, the Emergency Town Meeting Committee shall, in the open, immediately sort and count the ballots. Only the Emergency Town Meeting Committee shall be involved in the sorting and counting of ballots; no other person shall in any manner interfere. After counting, the Emergency Town Meeting Committee shall make a public declaration of the outcome of the vote. No ballot shall be received and counted after the outcome of the vote has been declared. A tie vote shall be resolved by a majority vote of the Emergency Town Meeting Committee. In the event of a tie vote of the Emergency Town Meeting Committee, the Ordinance shall be deemed to have been defeated.

Section 509. *Effect of the Vote.* If a majority of registered electors casting votes at the Meeting vote "no," the proposed Ordinance shall not take effect in Grant Township. If a majority of registered electors casting votes at the Meeting vote "yes," the proposed Ordinance shall immediately take effect in Grant Township. If a majority of registered electors casting votes at the Meeting vote "yes," the Township Board of Supervisors shall then take the necessary steps for the Ordinance to appear as a proposed amendment to the existing

Grant Township Home Rule Charter at the next available general, municipal, or primary election. If a majority of registered electors casting votes at the Meeting vote "yes," the Ordinance shall remain in effect only until the electors in Grant Township have the opportunity to vote on whether or not to amend the existing Charter with the Ordinance.

ARTICLE VI – CHARTER AMENDMENT

Section 601. Amendment. No proposed amendment to this Charter shall be withheld from the people's consideration on the basis that existing legal authority may consider the substance of the amendment to be "illegal" or "unconstitutional." Proposed amendments may only be withheld from the people's consideration if they have the effect of denying, abridging, or removing the rights of people, natural communities, or ecosystems, as recognized by this Charter. Amendments to this Charter shall be adopted pursuant to Pennsylvania law governing the amendment of Home Rule Charters.

Section 602. Severability. All provisions, sections, and subsections of this Charter are severable, and if any sub-section, clause, sentence, part, or provision thereof shall be held illegal, invalid, or unconstitutional by any court of competent jurisdiction, such decision of the court shall not affect, impair, or invalidate any of the remaining sections, clauses, sentences, parts, or provisions of this Charter. It is hereby declared to be the intent of the people that this Charter would have been adopted if such illegal, invalid, or unconstitutional section, clause, sentence, part, or provision had not been included herein.

ARTICLE VII – CALL FOR CONSTITUTIONAL CHANGES

Section 701. State and Federal Constitutional Changes. Through the adoption of this Charter, the people of Grant Township call for amendment of the Pennsylvania Constitution and the federal Constitution to recognize a right of local community self-government free from governmental preemption and nullification by corporate "rights" and powers.

ARTICLE VIII – DEFINITIONS

The following terms shall have the meanings defined in this section wherever they are used in this Charter:

"Charter" means the Grant Township Home Rule Charter.

"Corporation" for purposes of this Charter, includes any corporation, or other business entity, organized under the laws of any State or country.

"Depositing of waste from oil and gas extraction" includes, but is not limited to, the depositing, disposal, storage, beneficial use, treatment, recycling, injection, or introduction of materials including, but not limited to, brine, "produced water," "frack water," tailings, flowback, or any other waste or by-product of oil and gas extraction, by any means. The phrase shall also include the issuance of, or application for, any permit that would purport to allow these activities. This phrase shall not include temporary storage of oil and gas waste materials in the Township at existing well sites.

"Extraction" means the digging or drilling of a well for the purposes of exploring for, developing, or producing shale gas, oil, or other hydrocarbons.

"Person" means a natural person, or an association of natural persons, that does not qualify as a corporation under this Charter.

"Township" means Grant Township in Indiana County, Pennsylvania, its Township Board of Supervisors, or its representatives or agents.

Grant Township
Ordinance No. _____-2016

ESTABLISHING A RIGHT TO BE FREE FROM PROSECUTION FOR
NONVIOLENT DIRECT ACTION CARRIED OUT TO ENFORCE THE
GRANT TOWNSHIP HOME RULE CHARTER'S RIGHTS AND PRO-
HIBITIONS; LEGALIZING NONVIOLENT CIVIL DISOBEDIENCE TO
ACTIVITIES AUTHORIZED BY ILLEGITIMATE STATE AND FEDERAL
LAWS AND COURT RULINGS THAT VIOLATE THE RIGHTS AND PRO-
HIBITIONS OF THE GRANT TOWNSHIP HOME RULE CHARTER

Section 1. Authority. The Grant Township Board of Supervisors, on behalf of the people of Grant Township, adopt this Ordinance pursuant to the inherent authority of the people of Grant of local, community self-government, section 109 of the Grant Township home rule charter, and the authority of the people of Grant as recognized by the Pennsylvania Constitution's Declaration of Rights, the United States Constitution, and the principles codified by the Declaration of Independence.

Section 2. Right to Directly Enforce People's Rights. If a court fails to uphold the Grant Township home rule charter's limitations on corporate power, or otherwise fails to uphold the rights secured by Article One of the charter, the rights and prohibitions secured by the charter shall not be affected by that judicial failure, and any natural person may then enforce the rights and prohibitions of the charter through direct action. If enforcement through nonviolent direct action is commenced, this law shall prohibit any private or public actor from bringing criminal charges or filing any civil or other criminal action against those participating in nonviolent direct action. If filed in violation of this provision, the applicable court must dismiss the action promptly, without further filings being required of nonviolent direct action participants. "Nonviolent direct action" as used by this provision shall mean any nonviolent activities or actions carried out to directly enforce the rights and prohibitions contained within the Grant Township home rule charter.

ENACTED AND ORDAINED this ___ day of _____, 2016, by the Grant Township Board of Township Supervisors.

By: _____

_____

_____

Attest: _____

BARNSTEAD WATER RIGHTS AND LOCAL SELF-GOVERNMENT ORDINANCE
(New Hampshire)

Section 1. Name. The name of this Ordinance shall be the "Barnstead Water Rights and Local Self-Government Ordinance."

Section 2. Preamble and Purpose. We the People of the Town of Barnstead declare that water is essential for life, liberty, and the pursuit of happiness— both for people and for the ecological systems, which give life to all species.

We the People of the Town of Barnstead declare that we have the duty to safeguard the water both on and beneath the Earth's surface, and in the process, safeguard the rights of people within the community of Barnstead, and the rights of the ecosystems of which Barnstead is a part.

We the people of Barnstead declare that all of our water is held in the public trust as a common resource to be used for the benefit of Barnstead residents and of the natural ecosystems of which they are a part. We believe that the corporatization of water supplies in this community—placing the control of water in the hands of a corporate few, rather than the community—would constitute tyranny and usurpation; and that we are therefore duty bound, under the New Hampshire Constitution, to oppose such tyranny and usurpation.

That same duty requires us to recognize that two centuries' worth of governmental conferral of constitutional powers upon corporations has deprived people of the authority to govern their own communities, and requires us to take affirmative steps to remedy that usurpation of governing power.

Section 3. Authority. This Ordinance is adopted and enacted pursuant to the inherent, inalienable, and fundamental right of the citizens of the Town of Barnstead to self-government and under authority granted to the people of the Town by all relevant state and federal laws including, but not limited to the following:

Part First, Article 10 of the New Hampshire Constitution, which declares that government is instituted for the common benefit, protection and security of the whole community, and not for the private interest of any class of men;

Part First, Article 1 of the New Hampshire Constitution, which declares that government is founded upon the consent of the people and instituted for the common good;

The spirit of Part Second, Article 5 and Part Second, Article 83 of the New Hampshire Constitution, which subordinate corporations to the body politic;

NH RSA 31:39 I (a), (l) and III which, under powers and duties of Towns, permits bylaws for the care, protection, preservation of the commons; the ordering of their prudential affairs; and the enforcement of such bylaws by suitable penalties.

The Declaration of Independence, which declares that governments are instituted to secure people's rights, and that government derives its just powers from the consent of the governed;

The General Comment of the United Nations Covenant on Economic, Social, and Cultural Rights, which declares that "the human right to drinking water is fundamental to life and health. Sufficient and safe drinking water is a precondition to the realization of human rights."

Section 4. Statement of Law. No corporation or syndicate shall engage in water withdrawals in the Town of Barnstead. The term "corporation" means any corporation organized under the laws of any state of the United States or any country. The term "syndicate" includes any limited partnership, limited liability partnership, business trust, or Limited Liability Company organized under the laws of any state of the United States or any country. The term "engage" shall include, but not be limited to, the physical extraction of water, and the buying and/or selling of water extracted within the Town of Barnstead.

Section 5. Statement of Law. No corporation doing business within the Town of Barnstead shall be recognized as a "person" under the United States or New Hampshire Constitutions, or laws of the United States or New Hampshire, nor shall the corporation be afforded the protections of the Contracts Clause or Commerce Clause of the United States Constitution, or similar provisions found within the New Hampshire Constitution, within the Town of Barnstead.

Section 5.1. Rights. All residents of the Town of Barnstead possess a fundamental and inalienable right to access, use, consume, and preserve water drawn from the sustainable natural water cycles that provide water necessary to sustain life within the Town. Natural communities and ecosystems possess inalienable and fundamental rights to exist and flourish within the Town of Barnstead. Ecosystems shall include, but not be limited to, wetlands, streams, rivers, aquifers, and other water systems.

Section 6. Exceptions. The people of the Town of Barnstead hereby allow the following exceptions to the Statement of Law contained within §4 of this Ordinance:

(1) Municipal authorities established under the laws of the State of New Hampshire engaged in water withdrawals providing water only to residential and commercial users within the Town of Barnstead;

(2) Nonprofit educational and charitable corporations organized under state non-profit corporation law, and qualifying under §501(c)(3) of the federal Tax Code, which do not sell water withdrawn within the Town of Barnstead outside of the Town of Barnstead;

(3) Utility corporations operating under valid and express contractual provisions in agreements entered into between the Town of Barnstead and those utility corporations, for the provision of service within the Town of Barnstead;

(4) Corporations operating under valid and express contractual provisions in agreements entered into between residents of the Town of Barnstead and those corporations, when the withdrawn water is used solely for on-site residential, household, agricultural, or commercial facilities within the Town of Barnstead, as long as such commercial facilities do not withdraw water for sale outside of the Town of Barnstead, or purchase water withdrawn from the Town of Barnstead for sale outside of the Town.

Section 7. Enforcement. Any corporation planning to engage in water withdrawals within the Town of Barnstead must notify the Town of such activity at least sixty (60) days prior to engaging in water withdrawals. Such notification shall contain a claim to one of the exemptions listed in Section 6 of this Ordinance. Any violation of this Ordinance shall be considered a criminal summary offense, and will subject the Directors of the noncompliant corporation to joint and several liability with the corporation itself.

The Board of Selectmen of the Town of Barnstead authorizes a fine of up to $1,000.00 per violation. Each act of water withdrawal [and each day that water is withdrawn] shall be considered a separate violation of this Ordinance. The Board of Selectmen of the Town of Barnstead may also file an action in equity in the Belknap County Superior Court or any other Court of competent jurisdiction to abate any violation defined in Section 4 of this Ordinance. If the Selectmen of the Town of Barnstead fail to bring an action to enforce this Ordinance, any resident of the Town has standing in front of the Court for enforcement.

Section 7.1. Civil Rights: Any person acting under the authority of a permit issued by the Department of Environmental Services, any corporation operating under a State charter or certificate of authority to do business, or any director, officer, owner, or manager of a corporation operating under a State charter or certificate of authority to do business, who deprives any Town resident, natural community, or ecosystem of any rights, privileges, or immunities secured by this Warrant Article, the New Hampshire Constitution, the United States Constitution, or other laws, shall be liable to the party injured and shall be responsible for payment of compensatory and punitive damages and all costs of litigation to satisfy that liability, including, without limitation, expert and attorney's fees. Compensatory and punitive damages paid to remedy the violation of the rights of natural communities and ecosystems shall be paid to the Town of Barnstead for restoration of those natural communities and ecosystems.

Section 7.2. Environmental Protection: It shall be unlawful for any corporation or its directors, officers, owners, or managers to interfere with the rights of natural communities and ecosystems to exist and flourish, or to cause damage to those natural communities and ecosystems. The Town of Barnstead, along with any resident of the Town, shall have standing to seek declaratory, injunctive, compensatory, and punitive relief for damages caused to natural communities and ecosystems within the Town, regardless of the relation of those natural communities and ecosystems to Town residents or the Town itself. Town residents, natural communities, and ecosystems shall be considered to be "persons" for purposes of the enforcement of the civil rights of those residents, natural communities, and ecosystems.

Section 7.3. Civil Rights Enforcement: Any Town resident shall have standing and authority to bring an action under this Warrant Article's civil rights provisions, or under state and federal civil rights laws, for violations of the rights of natural communities, ecosystems, and Town residents, as recognized by this Warrant Article.

Section 7.4. Town Action Against Preemption. The foundation for the making and adoption of this law is the people's fundamental and inalienable right to govern themselves, and thereby secure rights to life, liberty, property, and pursuit of happiness. Any attempts to use county, state, or federal levels of government—judicial, legislative, or executive—to preempt, amend, alter, or overturn this Warrant Article or parts of this Warrant Article, or to intimidate the people of the Town of Barnstead or their elected officials, may require the Board of Selectmen to hold public meetings that explore the adoption of other measures that expand local control and the ability of residents to protect their fundamental and inalienable right to self-government. Such consideration may include actions to separate the municipality from the other levels of government used to preempt, amend, alter, or overturn the provisions of this Warrant Article or other levels of government used to intimidate the people of Barnstead or their elected officials.

Section 7.5. Strict Liability. Persons using corporations to engage in water withdrawal in a neighboring municipality shall be strictly liable for all harms caused to the health, safety, and welfare of the residents of Barnstead from those activities, and for all harms caused to ecosystems and natural communities within Barnstead.

Section 7.6. Liability. No permit, license, privilege or charter issued by any State or federal Regulatory Agency, Commission or Board to any person or any corporation operating under a State charter, or any director, officer, owner, or manager of a corporation operating under a State charter, which would violate the provisions of this Warrant Article or deprive any Barnstead resident, natural community, or ecosystem of any rights, privileges, or immunities secured by this Warrant Article, the New Hampshire Constitution, the United States Constitution, or other laws, shall be deemed valid within the Town of Barnstead. Additionally, any employee, agent or representative of any State or federal Regulatory Agency, Commission or Board who issues a permit, license, privilege or charter to any person or any corporation operating under a State charter, or any director, officer, owner, or manager of a corporation operating under a State charter, which would violate the provisions of this Warrant Article or deprive any resident, natural community, or ecosystem of any rights, privileges, or immunities secured by this Warrant Article, the New Hampshire Constitution, the United States Constitution, or other laws, shall be liable to the party injured and shall be responsible for payment of compensatory and punitive damages and all costs of litigation, including, without limitation, expert and attorney's fees. Compensatory and punitive damages paid to remedy the violation of the rights of natural communities and ecosystems shall be paid to the Town of Barnstead for restoration of those natural communities and ecosystems.

Section 7.7. Future Lost Profits. Within the Town of Barnstead, corporate claims to "future lost profits" shall not be considered property interests under the law, and thus, shall not be recoverable by corporations seeking those damages.

Section 8. Severability. The provisions of this Ordinance are severable, and if any section, clause, sentence, part, or provision thereof shall be held illegal, invalid or unconstitutional by any court of competent jurisdiction, such decision of the court shall not affect, impair, or invalidate any of the remaining sections, clauses, sentences, parts or provisions of this Ordinance. It is hereby declared to be the intent of the people of Barnstead that this Ordinance would have been adopted if such illegal, invalid, or unconstitutional section, clause, sentence, part, or provision had not been included herein.

Section 9. Effect. This Ordinance shall be effective immediately upon its enactment.

Tamaqua Borough, Schuylkill County, Pennsylvania
Ordinance No. _____ of 2006

AN ORDINANCE TO PROTECT THE HEALTH, SAFETY, AND GENERAL
WELFARE OF THE CITIZENS AND ENVIRONMENT OF TAMAQUA
BOROUGH BY BANNING CORPORATIONS FROM ENGAGING IN THE
LAND APPLICATION OF SEWAGE SLUDGE; BY BANNING PERSONS
FROM USING CORPORATIONS TO ENGAGE IN LAND APPLICATION
OF SEWAGE SLUDGE; BY PROVIDING FOR THE TESTING OF SEWAGE
SLUDGE PRIOR TO LAND APPLICATION IN THE BOROUGH; BY REMOV-
ING CONSTITUTIONAL POWERS FROM CORPORATIONS WITHIN
THE BOROUGH; BY RECOGNIZING AND ENFORCING THE RIGHTS OF
RESIDENTS TO DEFEND NATURAL COMMUNITIES AND ECOSYSTEMS;
AND BY OTHERWISE ADOPTING THE PENNSYLVANIA REGULATIONS
CONCERNING THE LAND APPLICATION OF SEWAGE SLUDGE

Section 1 – Name
This Ordinance shall be known and may be cited as the "Tamaqua Borough
Sewage Sludge Ordinance."

Section 2 – Authority
This Ordinance is enacted pursuant to the authority granted to Tamaqua
Borough by all relevant Federal and State laws and their corresponding regulations, and by the inherent right of the citizens of the Borough of Tamaqua
to self-government, including, without limitation, the following:

The Declaration of Independence, which declares that people are born
with "certain unalienable rights" and that governments are instituted among
people to secure those rights;

The Pennsylvania Constitution, Article 1, Section 2, which declares that
"all power is inherent in the people and all free governments are instituted for
their peace, safety, and happiness;"

The Pennsylvania Constitution, Article 1, Section 26, which declares
that "neither the Commonwealth nor any political subdivision thereof shall
deny to any person the enjoyment of any civil right;"

The Pennsylvania Constitution, Article I, Section 27, which provides
for the "preservation of the natural, scenic, historic, and esthetic values of the
environment;"

The Borough Code, Article XII, §1202(6), which establishes the authority of Borough governments in the Commonwealth to adopt Ordinances "as
may be necessary for the health, safety, morals, general welfare and cleanliness,
and the beauty, convenience, comfort and safety of the borough;"

The Borough Code, Article XII, §1202(28), which establishes the authority of Borough governments in the Commonwealth to adopt Ordinances "to

prohibit, within the borough, the carrying on of any manufacture, art, trade, or business which may be noxious or offensive to the inhabitants;"

The Borough Code, Article XII, §1202(74), which establishes the general power of Borough governments in the Commonwealth to make and adopt Ordinances that "may be expedient or necessary for the proper management, care and control of the borough and its finances, and the maintenance of peace, good government, safety and welfare of the borough and its trade, commerce and manufactures;"

The Solid Waste Management Act, 35 P.S. § 6018.101 *et seq.*, which preserves the rights and remedies of municipalities concerning solid waste within their borders;

Municipal Waste Regulations, 25 Pa. Code §§ 271 and 275, *et seq.*; and

Land Application of Sewage Sludge, 40 C.F.R. Part 503.

Section 3 – Findings and Purpose

In support of enactment of this Ordinance, the Borough Council of Tamaqua Borough finds and declares that:

The land application of sewage sludge in Tamaqua Borough poses a significant threat to the health, safety, and welfare of the citizens and environment of Tamaqua Borough.

In April 2002, the Inspector General of the Environmental Protection Agency (EPA), which oversees state sewage sludge regulations, issued a report in which it concluded, "EPA cannot assure the public that current land application [of sewage sludge] practices are protective of human health and the environment." Among the Inspector General's concerns were the following: "failure to properly manage sludge may have adverse effects on human health and the environment"; "EPA does not have an effective program of ensuring compliance with land application requirements"; and state officials have criticized the lack of EPA oversight, staffing, and commitment toward ensuring the safety of land applied sludge.

In 1994, eleven-year-old Tony Behun from Rush Township, Centre County, Pennsylvania, died from a staph infection shortly after being exposed to sewage sludge. The following year, seventeen-year-old Daniel Pennock from Reading, Pennsylvania, died from a staph infection shortly after being exposed to sewage sludge. The U.S. Environmental Protection Agency (EPA) recognizes staph as a potential pathogenic component of sewage sludge.

In spite of these risks, Tamaqua Borough has been rendered powerless by the state and federal government to prohibit the land application of sewage sludge by persons that comply with all applicable laws and regulations.

In order to protect the health, safety, and welfare of the residents of Tamaqua Borough, the soil, groundwater, and surface water, the environment and its flora and fauna, and the practice of sustainable agriculture, the Borough finds it necessary to ban corporations and other limited liability entities from engaging in the land application of sewage sludge. It is recognized that a small number of waste management corporations control the vast majority of sludge hauling and land application, and that corporate concentration enables those corporations to define waste management practices at the State level to the detriment of municipal communities. It is also recognized that limited liability shields prevent financial recovery (and accountability) for damages caused by business entities because limited liability insulates the persons managing the corporation from harms caused by their decisions. Finally, the Borough recognizes that corporations wielding government-conferred constitutional powers against the municipal government renders the Borough Council unable to guarantee to its citizens a republican form of government in the Borough.

In order to protect the health, safety, and welfare of the residents of Tamaqua Borough, the soil, groundwater, and surface water, the environment and its flora and fauna, and the practice of sustainable agriculture, it is necessary to test each load of sewage sludge to be applied by persons before it is land applied within the Borough to determine if the level of pollutants, pathogens, or vector attractants exceed the levels allowed under applicable laws and regulations.

DEP does not possess sufficient funding or personnel to ensure that persons land applying sewage sludge in Tamaqua Borough are doing so in compliance with state laws and regulations, so Tamaqua Borough must have the option of enforcing those laws and regulations itself.

Tamaqua Borough's cost of testing sewage sludge prior to land application shall be borne by those persons land applying sewage sludge in the Borough.

Section 4 – Interpretation

Anyone interpreting, implementing, or applying this Ordinance shall give priority to the findings and purposes stated in Sections 2 and 3 over such considerations as economy, efficiency, and scheduling factors.

Section 5 – Definitions

The following terms shall have the meanings defined in this section wherever they are used in this Ordinance.

Beneficial Use: Use or reuse of residual waste or material derived from residual waste for commercial, industrial, or governmental purposes where the use or reuse does not harm or threaten public health, safety, welfare, or the environment, or the use or reuse of processed municipal waste for any purpose where the use or reuse does not harm or threaten public health, safety, welfare, or the environment. (*See* 25 Pa. Code Chapter 271, Subchapter A, § 271.1.)

Borough: Tamaqua Borough in Schuylkill County, Pennsylvania, its Borough Council, or its representatives or agents.

Corporation: Any corporation organized under the laws of any state of the United States or under the laws of any country. The term shall also include any limited partnership, limited liability partnership, business trust, or limited liability company organized under the laws of any state of the United States or under the laws of any country, and any other business entity that possesses State-conferred limited liability attributes for its owners, directors, officers, and/or managers. The term shall also include a municipality or municipal authority. The term shall also include any business entity in which one or more owners or partners is a corporation or other entity in which owners, directors, officers and/or managers possess limited liability attributes.

DEP: The Pennsylvania Department of Environmental Protection.

Laboratory or Qualified Laboratory: A facility that tests sewage sludge samples for pollutants, pathogens, and vector attractants in compliance with DEP regulations, including, without limitation, those regulations (*see* 25 Pa. Code § 271.906) that dictate approved methodologies for conducting such tests.

Land Applicant or Sewage Sludge Applicant: Any person responsible for complying with all Federal, State, and local laws and regulations concerning the land application of sewage sludge.

Land Application or Land Apply: The spraying or spreading of sewage sludge onto the land surface for beneficial use; the injection of sewage sludge below the land surface for beneficial use; or the incorporation of sewage sludge into the soil for beneficial use so that the sewage sludge can either condition the soil or fertilize crops for vegetation grown in the soil. (*See* 25 Pa. Code Chapter 271, Subchapter J, § 271.907.) The term shall also include the spraying, spreading, injection, or incorporation of sewage sludge onto, into, or below the land surface for reclamation of previously mined lands.

Ordinance: The Tamaqua Borough Sewage Sludge Ordinance.

Person: A natural person, or an association of natural persons that does not qualify as a corporation under this Ordinance.

Sewage Sludge or Sludge: Liquid or solid sludge and other residue from a municipal sewage collection and treatment system, and liquid or solid sludge and other residue from septic and holding tank pumpings from commercial, industrial, or residential establishments. The term includes material derived from sewage sludge. The term does not include ash generated during the firing of sewage sludge in a sewage sludge incinerator, grit and screenings generated during preliminary treatment of sewage sludge at a municipal sewage collection and treatment system, or grit, screenings, or inorganic objects from septic and holding tank pumpings. (*See* 25 Pa. Code Chapter 271, Subchapter A, § 271.1.)

Sewage Sludge Applicant: *See* Land Applicant

SOUR: Specific oxygen uptake rate, which is the mass of oxygen consumed per unit time per unit mass of total solids (dry weight basis) in the sewage sludge.

Substantially Owned or Controlled: A person, corporation, or other entity substantially owns or controls another person, corporation, or other entity if it has the ability to evade the intent of Section 11.6 of this Ordinance by using that person, corporation, or other entity to land apply sewage sludge in Tamaqua Borough.

Truckload: A load containing a maximum of approximately 23 (twenty-three) tons of sewage sludge, based upon Tamaqua Borough's understanding that sewage sludge for land application typically is delivered in tri-axle trucks that can hold approximately that amount of sewage sludge.

Section 6 – Adoption of State Regulations

Tamaqua Borough hereby adopts as local law the Pennsylvania regulations concerning the land application of sewage sludge, including without limitation those codified at 25 Pa. Code §§ 271 and 275, *et seq.*, as amended, to the extent that those regulations permit persons, but not corporations, to engage in land application of sewage sludge under those regulations.

Section 7 – Statements of Law

Section 7.1: It shall be unlawful for any person, corporation, or other entity to violate in Tamaqua Borough the Pennsylvania regulations concerning the land application of sewage sludge, including without limitation those codified at 25 Pa. Code §§ 271 and 275, *et seq.*, as amended.

Section 7.2: It shall be unlawful for any person to land apply sewage sludge in Tamaqua Borough without first complying with the requirements in section 8 of this Ordinance.

Section 7.3: It shall be unlawful for any corporation to engage in the land application of sludge within the Borough of Tamaqua. It shall be unlawful for any person to assist a corporation to engage in the land application of sewage sludge within Tamaqua Borough.

Section 7.4: It shall be unlawful for any director, officer, owner, or manager of a corporation to use a corporation to engage in the land application of sludge within the Borough of Tamaqua.

Section 7.5: Within the Borough of Tamaqua, corporations engaged in the land application of sludge, dredged material, or any other type of waste as defined under Title 25, §271.1 of the Pennsylvania Code, shall not be "persons" under the United States or Pennsylvania Constitutions, or under the laws of the United States, Pennsylvania, or Tamaqua Borough, and so shall not have the rights of persons under those constitutions and laws. In addition, within the Borough of Tamaqua, no corporation engaged in the land application of sludge, dredged material, or any other type of waste as defined under Title 25, §271.1 of the Pennsylvania Code, shall be afforded the protections of the Contracts Clause or Commerce Clause of the United States Constitution, or similar provisions from the Pennsylvania Constitution.

Section 7.6: It shall be unlawful for any corporation or its directors, officers, owners, or managers to interfere with the existence and flourishing of natural communities or ecosystems, or to cause damage to those natural communities and ecosystems. The Borough of Tamaqua, along with any resident of the Borough, shall have standing to seek declaratory, injunctive, and compensatory relief for damages caused to natural communities and ecosystems within the Borough, regardless of the relation of those natural communities and ecosystems to Borough residents or the Borough itself. Borough residents, natural communities, and ecosystems shall be considered to be "persons" for purposes of the enforcement of the civil rights of those residents, natural communities, and ecosystems.

Section 7.7: All residents of Tamaqua Borough possess a fundamental and inalienable right to a healthy environment, which includes the right to unpolluted air, water, soils, flora, and fauna. All residents of the Borough possess a fundamental and inalienable right to the integrity of their bodies, and thus have a right to be free from unwanted invasions of their bodies by pollutants.

Section 8 – Application and Testing Requirements

Before each and every truckload of sewage sludge is land applied in Tamaqua Borough by a person, the sewage sludge applicant must do the following:

Section 8.1: Complete and submit to the Borough a written application in form and number provided by the Borough and containing the name and address of the sewage sludge applicant, the name and address of the landowner on whose land the sewage sludge is to be land applied, the location of the land on which the sewage sludge is to be land applied, and a copy of all DEP and other applicable state and federal permits pertaining to the land application.

Section 8.2: Provide Tamaqua Borough with written proof of the Class of sewage sludge to be land applied. If the sludge is Class A, provide Tamaqua Borough with written proof of the Alternative in 25 Pa. Code § 271.932(a) under which the sludge qualifies as Class A. If the sludge is Class B, provide

Tamaqua Borough with written proof of the Alternative in 25 Pa. Code §
271.932(b) under which the sludge qualifies as Class B. For all Classes of
sludge, provide Tamaqua Borough with written proof of the Alternative in
25 Pa. Code § 933(b) under which the sludge purportedly satisfies DEP
vector attraction requirements. The purpose of this subsection is to confirm
the Class of sludge to be applied and to identify the testing that Tamaqua
Borough must conduct on the sewage sludge and the requisite testing and
collection fees under Section 8.4 of this Ordinance.

Section 8.3: Arrange for and allow Tamaqua Borough to collect the necessary
sewage sludge samples from the truckload to be land applied to have a qualified laboratory test the sludge for pollutants, pathogens, and vector attractants regulated by DEP at 25 Pa. Code § 271.914 (pollutants), § 271.932
(pathogens), § 271.933 (vector attractants), and at all other applicable state
and federal regulations, as amended.

Section 8.4: Pay Tamaqua Borough the testing and collection fees identified
below and, when indicated, provide Tamaqua Borough with the written proof
requested below.

Pollutants:

For all classes of sewage sludge, the testing fee for
pollutants under 25 Pa. Code § 271.914(a)(1) will
be determined based upon quotes from one or
more qualified laboratories at the time of testing.

Pathogens:

For Class B sludge under Alternative 1 of 25 Pa.
Code § 271.932(b), the testing fee to test seven
samples for fecal coliform will be determined based
upon quotes from one or more qualified laboratories at the time of testing.

For Class B sludge under Alternatives 2 and 3 of
25 Pa. Code § 271.932(b), the sewage sludge applicant shall submit written proof that the sludge to
be land applied has been treated as required under
the applicable Alternative.

Vector Attractants:

For sewage sludge that purportedly satisfies vector attraction requirements under 25 Pa. Code §
271.933(b)(1), (2), or (3), the testing fee for mass
of volatile solids will be determined based upon
quotes from one or more qualified laboratories at
the time of testing.

For sewage sludge that purportedly satisfies vector attraction requirements under 25 Pa. Code § 271.933(b)(4), the testing fee for SOUR will be determined based upon quotes from one or more qualified laboratories at the time of testing.

For sewage sludge that purportedly satisfies vector attraction requirements under 25 Pa. Code § 271.933(b)(5), (6), (7), (8), (9), or (10), the sewage sludge applicant shall submit written proof that the sludge to be land applied satisfies the requirements under the applicable Alternative.

Collection:

For all classes of sewage sludge, the administrative fee for collection and transportation of the sewage sludge samples for testing, and for handling the application, is $50.00 per truckload of sewage sludge to be land applied.

Section 8.5: Store the sewage sludge pursuant to all applicable DEP, federal, and state regulations (including without limitation those at 25 Pa. Code §275.204 and 25 Pa. Code Chapter 285) until the Borough notifies the sewage sludge applicant whether it may land apply the sewage sludge in Tamaqua Borough. The sewage sludge applicant shall notify Tamaqua Borough of the location of the stored sludge and the identity of the container storing the sludge, in a manner sufficient to enable the Borough to verify that the stored sludge is the same sludge being considered for land application.

Section 8.6: If the land applicant does not receive permission to land apply the sewage sludge in Tamaqua Borough, it shall follow all applicable state and federal regulations for handling and disposing of sewage sludge that may not be land applied.

Section 8.7: If the land applicant receives notice that it is allowed to land apply the sewage sludge in Tamaqua Borough, it shall do so in compliance with all applicable federal, state, and local laws and regulations.

Section 9 – Testing Procedures

When Tamaqua Borough receives all of the following—a complete application pursuant to section 8.1 of this Ordinance; all information required under Section 8.2 of this Ordinance; and all testing and collection fees and written proofs required under Section 8.4 of this Ordinance—it shall do the following:

Section 9.1: Collect the necessary sewage sludge samples for testing by a qualified laboratory for compliance with DEP's pollutant regulations at 25 Pa. Code § 271.914, pathogen regulations for Class B sludge at § 271.932, vector attractant regulations at § 271.933, and all other applicable state and federal regulations, as amended. The Borough shall instruct the laboratory to conduct the tests in compliance with all DEP regulations for testing sewage sludge to be land applied under the beneficial use program.

Section 9.2: Inform the sewage sludge applicant of the results of testing conducted pursuant to Section 9.1 within seventy-two (72) hours after receiving the results.

Section 9.3: If the testing reveals that the sewage sludge contains levels of pollutants, pathogens, or vector attractants that violate DEP regulations at 25 Pa. Code § 271.914 (pollutants), § 271.932 (pathogens), § 271.933 (vector attractants), or any other federal or state laws or regulations, as amended, the Borough shall deny permission for the sewage sludge to be land applied in Tamaqua Borough. Otherwise, the Borough shall grant permission for the land application.

Section 10 – Administration
This Ordinance shall be administered by Tamaqua Borough. The Borough may, but is not required to, administer and enforce, at Borough expense (except as provided in section 8.4 of this Ordinance), any and all regulations that it has adopted pursuant to Section 6 of this Ordinance.

Section 11 – Enforcement

Section 11.1: Tamaqua Borough shall enforce this Ordinance by an action brought before a district justice in the same manner provided for the enforcement of summary offenses under the Pennsylvania Rules of Criminal Procedure. (*See* 53 P.S. § 66601(c.1)(2).)

Section 11.2: Any person, corporation, or other entity that violates any provision of this Ordinance shall be guilty of a summary offense and, upon conviction thereof by a district justice, shall be sentenced to pay a fine of $750 for first-time violations, $1000 for second-time violations, and $1000 for each subsequent violation, and shall be imprisoned to the extent allowed by law for the punishment of summary offenses. (*See* 53 P.S. § 66601(c.1)(2).)

Section 11.3: A separate offense shall arise for each day or portion thereof in which a violation occurs and for each section of this Ordinance that is found to be violated. (*See* 53 P.S. § 66601(c.1)(5).)

Section 11.4: Tamaqua Borough may also enforce this Ordinance through an action in equity brought in the Court of Common Pleas of Schuylkill County. (*See* 53 P.S. § 66601 (c.1)(4).) In such an action, Tamaqua Borough shall be entitled to recover all costs of litigation, including, without limitation, expert and attorney's fees.

Section 11.5: All monies collected for violation of this Ordinance shall be paid to the Treasurer of Tamaqua Borough.

Section 11.6: Any person, corporation, or other entity that violates, or is convicted of violating this Ordinance, two or more times shall be permanently prohibited from land applying sewage sludge in Tamaqua Borough. This prohibition applies to that person's, corporation's, or other entity's parent, sister, and successor companies, subsidiaries, and alter egos, and to any person, corporation, or other entity substantially owned or controlled by the person, corporation, or other entity (including its officers, directors, or owners) that twice violates this Ordinance, and to any person, corporation, or other entity that substantially owns or controls the person, corporation, or other entity that twice violates this Ordinance.

Section 11.7: Any Borough resident shall have the authority to enforce this Ordinance through an action in equity brought in the Court of Common Pleas of Schuylkill County. In such an action, the resident shall be entitled to recover all costs of litigation, including, without limitation, expert and attorney's fees.

Section 12 – Civil Rights Enforcement

Section 12.1: Any person acting under the authority of a permit issued by the Department of Environmental Protection, any corporation operating under a State charter, or any director, officer, owner, or manager of a corporation operating under a State charter, who deprives any Borough resident, natural community, or ecosystem of any rights, privileges, or immunities secured by this Ordinance, the Pennsylvania Constitution, the United States Constitution, or other laws, shall be liable to the party injured and shall be responsible for payment of compensatory and punitive damages and all costs of litigation, including, without limitation, expert and attorney's fees. Compensatory and punitive damages paid to remedy the violation of the rights of natural communities and ecosystems shall be paid to Tamaqua Borough for restoration of those natural communities and ecosystems.

Section 12.2: Any Borough resident shall have standing and authority to bring an action under this Ordinance's civil rights provisions, or under state and federal civil rights laws, for violations of the rights of natural communities, ecosystems, and Borough residents, as recognized by sections 7.6 and 7.7 of this Ordinance.

Section 13 – Effective Date and Existing DEP Permitholders
This Ordinance shall be effective five (5) days after the date of its enactment, at which point the Ordinance shall apply to any and all land applications of sewage sludge in Tamaqua Borough regardless of the date of the applicable DEP permits.

Section 14 – People's Right to Self-Government
The foundation for the making and adoption of this law is the people's fundamental and inalienable right to govern themselves, and thereby secure their rights to life, liberty, and pursuit of happiness. Any attempts to use other units and levels of government to preempt, amend, alter, or overturn this Ordinance, or parts of this Ordinance, shall require the Borough Council to hold public meetings that explore the adoption of other measures that expand local control and the ability of residents to protect their fundamental and inalienable right to self-government.

Section 15 – Severability
The provisions of this Ordinance are severable. If any court of competent jurisdiction decides that any section, clause, sentence, part, or provision of this Ordinance is illegal, invalid, or unconstitutional, such decision shall not affect, impair, or invalidate any of the remaining sections, clauses, sentences, parts, or provisions of the Ordinance. The Borough Council of Tamaqua Borough hereby declares that in the event of such a decision, and the determination that the court's ruling is legitimate, it would have enacted this Ordinance even without the section, clause, sentence, part, or provision that the court decides is illegal, invalid, or unconstitutional.

Section 16 – Repealer
All inconsistent provisions of prior Ordinances adopted by the Borough of Tamaqua are hereby repealed, but only to the extent necessary to remedy the inconsistency.

ENACTED AND ORDAINED this ___ day of _____, 2006, by the Borough Council of Tamaqua Borough.

By: _____

_____

_____

Attest: _____

Ordinance supplementing the Pittsburgh Code, Title Six, Conduct, Article 1 Regulated Rights and actions, by adding Chapter 618 entitled Marcellus Shale Natural Gas Drilling.

ARTICLE VI: CONDUCT

CHAPTER 618: MARCELLUS SHALE NATURAL GAS DRILLING

618.01 Findings and intent
618.02 Definitions
618.03 Statements of law—rights of Pittsburgh residents and the natural environment
618.04 Statements of law—prohibitions and corporate legal services
618.05 Enforcement
618.06 Effective date and existing DEP permit holders
618.07 People's Right to Self-Government
618.08 Severability
618.09 Repealer

Whereas, this is an ordinance to protect the health, safety, and welfare of residents and neighborhoods of Pittsburgh by banning the commercial extraction of natural gas within the city; and

Whereas, this ordinance establishes a Bill of Rights for Pittsburgh residents and removes legal powers from gas extraction corporations within the City; and

Whereas, this Ordinance shall be known and may be cited as "Pittsburgh's Community Protection from Natural Gas Extraction Ordinance;" and

Whereas, this Ordinance is enacted pursuant to the inherent right of the residents of the City of Pittsburgh to govern their own community, including, without limitation, the Declaration of Independence's declaration that governments are instituted to secure the rights of people, and the Pennsylvania Constitution's recognition that "all power is inherent in the people."

618.01 FINDINGS AND INTENT

The City Council of Pittsburgh finds that the commercial extraction of natural gas in the urban environment of Pittsburgh poses a significant threat to the health, safety, and welfare of residents and neighborhoods within the City. Moreover, widespread environmental and human health impacts have resulted from commercial gas extraction in other areas. Regulating the activity of commercial gas extraction automatically means allowing commercial gas extraction to occur within the City, thus allowing the deposit of toxins into the air, soil, water, environment, and the bodies of residents within our City.

Meaningful regulatory limitations and prohibitions concerning Marcellus Shale natural gas extraction, along with zoning and land use provisions, are barred because they conflict with certain legal powers claimed by resource extraction corporations. The City Council recognizes that environmental and economic sustainability cannot be achieved if the rights of municipal majorities are routinely overridden by corporate minorities claiming certain legal powers.

The City Council believes that the protection of residents, neighborhoods, and the natural environment constitutes the highest and best use of the police powers that this municipality possesses. The City Council also believes that local legislation that embodies the interests of the community is mandated by the doctrine of the consent of the governed, and the right to local, community self-government. Thus, the City Council hereby adopts this ordinance, which bans commercial extraction of Marcellus Shale natural gas within the City of Pittsburgh, creates a Bill of Rights for the residents and communities of the City, and removes certain legal powers from gas extraction corporations operating within the City of Pittsburgh.

618.02 DEFINITIONS

(a)   "Natural Gas" shall mean any gaseous substance, either combustible or noncombustible, which is produced in a natural state from the earth and which maintains a gaseous or rarified state at standard temperature or pressure conditions, and/or gaseous components or vapors occurring in or derived from petroleum or natural gas.

(b)   "Extraction" shall mean the digging or drilling of a well for the purposes of exploring for, developing or producing natural gas or other hydrocarbons.

(c)   "Corporations," for purposes of this ordinance, shall include any corporation, limited partnership, limited liability partnership, business trust, or limited liability company organized under the laws of any state of the United States or under the laws of any country, and any other business entity that possesses State-conferred limited liability attributes for its owners, directors, officers, and/or managers.

618.03 STATEMENTS OF LAW – RIGHTS OF PITTSBURGH RESIDENTS AND THE NATURAL ENVIRONMENT

(a)   Right to Water. All residents, natural communities and ecosystems in Pittsburgh possess a fundamental and inalienable right to sustainably access, use, consume, and preserve water drawn from natural water cycles that provide water necessary to sustain life within the City.

(b)   Rights of Natural Communities. Natural communities and ecosystems, including, but not limited to, wetlands, streams, rivers, aquifers, and other water systems, possess inalienable and fundamental rights to exist and flourish within the City of Pittsburgh. Residents of the City shall possess legal standing to enforce those rights on behalf of those natural communities and ecosystems.

(c)   Right to Self-Government. All residents of Pittsburgh possess the fundamental and inalienable right to a form of governance where they live which recognizes that all power is inherent in the people, that all free governments are founded on the people's authority and consent, and that corporate entities and their directors and managers shall not enjoy special privileges or powers under the law which make community majorities subordinate to them.

(d)   People as Sovereign. The City of Pittsburgh shall be the governing authority responsible to, and governed by, the residents of the City. Use of the "City of Pittsburgh" municipal corporation by the sovereign people of the City to make law shall not be construed to limit or surrender the sovereign authority or immunities of the people to a municipal corporation that is subordinate to them in all respects at all times. The people at all times enjoy and retain an inalienable and indefeasible right to self-governance in the community where they reside.

618.04 STATEMENTS OF LAW – PROHIBITIONS AND CORPORATE LEGAL PRIVILEGES

(a)   It shall be unlawful for any corporation to engage in the extraction of natural gas within the City of Pittsburgh, with the exception of gas wells installed and operating at the time of enactment of this Ordinance.

(b)   Corporations in violation of the prohibition against natural gas extraction, or seeking to engage in natural gas extraction shall not have the rights of "persons" afforded by the United States and Pennsylvania Constitutions, nor shall those corporations be afforded the protections of the commerce or contracts clauses within the United States Constitution or corresponding sections of the Pennsylvania Constitution.

(c)   Corporations engaged in the extraction of natural gas shall not possess the authority or power to enforce State or federal preemptive law against the people of the City of Pittsburgh, or to challenge or overturn municipal ordinances adopted by the City Council of Pittsburgh.

(d)   No permit, license, privilege or charter issued by any State or federal agency, Commission or Board to any person or any corporation operating under a State charter, or any director, officer, owner, or manager of a corporation operating under a State charter, which would violate the prohibitions of this Ordinance or deprive any City resident(s), natural community, or ecosystem of any rights, privileges, or immunities secured by this Ordinance, the Pennsylvania Constitution, the United States Constitution, or other laws, shall be deemed valid within the City of Pittsburgh.

618.05 ENFORCEMENT

(a)   Any person, corporation, or other entity that violates any prohibition of this Ordinance shall be guilty of a summary offense and, upon conviction thereof by a district justice, shall be sentenced to pay the maximum fine allowable under State law for that violation, and shall be imprisoned to the extent allowed by law. A separate offense shall arise for each day or portion thereof in which a violation occurs and for each section of this Ordinance found to be violated.

(b)   The City of Pittsburgh may also enforce this Ordinance through an action in equity brought in the Court of Common Pleas of Allegheny County. In such an action, the City of Pittsburgh shall be entitled to recover all costs of litigation, including, without limitation, expert and attorney's fees.

(c)   Any City resident shall have the authority to enforce this Ordinance through an action in equity brought in the Court of Common Pleas of Allegheny County. In such an action, the resident shall be entitled to recover all costs of litigation, including, without limitation, expert and attorney's fees.

618.06 EFFECTIVE DATE AND EXISTING DEP PERMIT HOLDERS

(a) This Ordinance shall be effective upon the mayors signature or (10) days after the date of its enactment, at which point the Ordinance shall apply to any and all commercial extractions of natural gas in Pittsburgh regardless of the day of any applicable DEP permits.

618.07 PEOPLE'S RIGHT TO SELF-GOVERNMENT

(a) The foundation for the making and adoption of this law is the people's fundamental and inalienable right to govern themselves, and thereby secure their rights to life, liberty, and pursuit of happiness. Any attempts to use other units and levels of government to preempt, amend, alter, or overturn this Ordinance, or parts of this Ordinance, shall require the City Council to hold public meetings that explore the adoption of other measures that expand local control and the ability of residents to protect their fundamental and inalienable right to self-government. Such consideration may include actions to separate the municipality from the other levels of government used to preempt, amend, alter, or overturn the provisions of this Ordinance or other levels of government used to intimidate the people of the City of Pittsburgh or their elected officials.

618.08 SEVERABILITY

(a) The provisions of this Ordinance are severable. If any court of competent jurisdiction decides that any section, clause, sentence, part, or provision of this Ordinance is illegal, invalid, or unconstitutional, such decision shall not affect, impair, or invalidate any of the remaining sections, clauses, sentences, parts, or provisions of the Ordinance. The City Council of Pittsburgh hereby declares that in the event of such a decision, and the determination that the court's ruling is legitimate, it would have enacted this Ordinance even without the section, clause, sentence, part, or provision that the court decides is illegal, invalid, or unconstitutional.

618.09 REPEALER

(a) All inconsistent provisions of prior Ordinances adopted by the City of Pittsburgh are hereby repealed, but only to the extent necessary to remedy the inconsistency.

Proposition 1
Community Bill of Rights, Spokane, Washington

First. **Neighborhood Residents Have the Right to Determine the Future of Their Neighborhoods.**

Neighborhood majorities shall have the right to approve all zoning changes proposed for their neighborhood involving significant commercial, industrial, or residential development. Proposed commercial or industrial development shall be deemed significant if it exceeds ten thousand square feet, and proposed residential development shall be deemed significant if it exceeds twenty units and its construction is not financed by governmental funds allocated for low-income housing. It shall be the responsibility of the proposer of the zoning change to acquire the approval of the neighborhood majority, and the zoning change shall not be effective without it. Neighborhood majorities shall also have a right to reject significant commercial, industrial, or residential development which is incompatible with the provisions of the City's Comprehensive Plan or this Charter. Approval of a zoning change or rejection of proposed development under this section shall become effective upon the submission of a petition to the City containing the valid signatures of a majority of registered voters who reside within that neighborhood approving the zoning change or rejecting the proposed development, in a petition generally conforming to the referendum provisions of the Spokane municipal code.

Second. **The Right to a Healthy Spokane River and Aquifer.**

The Spokane River, its tributaries, and the Spokane Valley-Rathdrum Prairie Aquifer possess inalienable rights to exist and flourish, which shall include the right to sustainable recharge, flows sufficient to protect native fish habitat, and clean water. The City of Spokane and any resident of the City or group of residents have standing to enforce and protect these rights.

Third. **Employees Have the Right to Constitutional Protections in the Workplace.**

Employees shall possess United States and Washington Bill of Rights' constitutional protections in the workplace within the

City of Spokane, and workers in unionized workplaces shall possess the right to collective bargaining.

Fourth.   **Corporate Powers Shall be Subordinate to People's Rights.**

Corporations and other business entities which violate the rights secured by this Charter shall not be deemed to be "persons," nor possess any other legal rights, privileges, powers, or protections which would interfere with the enforcement of rights enumerated by this Charter.

Spokane Worker Bill of Rights

WHEREAS, the people of the City of Spokane wish to build a healthy, sustainable, economically just, and democratic community; and

WHEREAS, the people of the City of Spokane believe in the rights of workers to receive (1) a decent and fair family wage, (2) equitable pay regardless of personal traits, qualities, or characteristics, and (3) just cause for termination from employment; and

WHEREAS, the people of the City of Spokane believe these rights are superior to competing rights claimed by corporations; and

WHEREAS, the people of the City of Spokane have adopted a Comprehensive Plan for the City of Spokane, which envisions, among other items, income equity, living wages, and sustainable economic strategies, but the people recognize that the Comprehensive Plan is not legally enforceable in many important respects; and

WHEREAS, the people of the City of Spokane wish to create a Worker Bill of Rights, which would, among other goals, establish legally enforceable rights for workers to protect the local economy and build the people's vision of a healthy, sustainable, economically just, and democratic community.

Section 120. Worker Bill of Rights

A.   Worker Bill of Rights

1.   **Right to a Family Wage.** Workers in the City of Spokane have a right to a family wage. Workers employed by an employer with one hundred fifty (150) or more full-time equivalent workers shall be paid, at minimum, a family wage for work performed. The employer requirement to pay a family wage shall not apply to workers in a ninety (90) day or less probationary period, in an internship if enrolled in school, or when enrolled in a Washington state certified apprenticeship program.

2.   **Right to Equal Pay.** All workers in the City of Spokane have a right to equal pay for equal work. No employer may provide different wage rates or other compensation to workers who are performing jobs that require equal skill, effort, and responsibility because of the worker's gender, sexual orientation, gender identity, gender expression, familial status, race, ethnicity, national origin, citizenship, economic class, religion, age or developmental, mental, or physical ability.

3.   **Right Not to be Wrongfully Terminated.** Workers in the City of Spokane have a right to be free from wrongful termination.

Employers with ten (10) or more full-time equivalent workers shall not terminate a worker except for just cause, unless the worker is in a ninety (90) day or less probationary period, is enrolled in a Washington state certified apprenticeship program, or is expressly hired for a particular project and the project has ended. The term "just cause" shall be interpreted in accordance with established, common law principles of collective bargaining and labor relations, as developed by labor arbitration decisions, and an employer seeking to terminate a worker for just cause must demonstrate:

a. Timely and adequate work performance warnings and opportunities to correct work performance, unless the misconduct of the worker is serious enough to warrant immediate termination, such as criminal activity at work;

b. A fair, objective, and non-discriminatory termination process, where the worker has an opportunity to be heard in opposition to the termination; and

c. The termination is for work performance reasons, unless the employer can demonstrate that a layoff of a worker is necessary for economic hardship.

If a court finds a worker has been wrongfully terminated, the affected worker shall receive compensation in the form of back pay, reinstatement, attorney fees, costs, and damages.

4. **Corporate Powers Subordinate To People's Rights.** Corporations that violate, or seek to violate, this section shall not be deemed to be "persons" to the extent that such treatment would interfere with the rights enumerated in this section, nor shall corporations possess any other legal rights that would interfere with the rights enumerated by this section, including standing to challenge this section in court, the power to assert state or federal preemptive laws in an attempt to overturn this section, and the power to assert that the people of this municipality lack the authority to adopt this section.

B. Definitions

1. "Corporation" means any corporation, limited partnership, limited liability partnership, business trust, limited liability company, or other business entity, organized under the laws of any State of the United States or under the laws of any country.

2.   "Employer" means government and any business having, or required to have, a business license from the City of Spokane. For the purposes of determining the number of employees of a particular employer, a corporation, as defined in Section 2(a), that is doing business at more than one location shall be treated as a single employer, all franchisees and subsidiary corporations shall be treated as a single employer with the franchisor and parent corporation, and employees employed outside of the City of Spokane shall be counted for the purposes of determining the total number of full-time equivalent workers.

3.   "Family wage" means a wage that provides for basic needs and a limited ability to deal with future emergencies without the need of public assistance. The City of Spokane shall calculate the family wage to include, but not be limited to, basic necessities such as food, housing, utilities, transportation, health care, childcare, clothing and other personal items, emergency savings, and taxes. The City shall calculate the family wage rate based on a household size of two with one person employed and the family wage rate shall not be less than the Self-Sufficiency Standard for Washington State 2014, as adjusted for inflation. The City shall calculate the initial family wage within six months after the effective date of this section, and shall adjust the family wage each January 1st thereafter to reflect the change in the Consumer Price Index for the Spokane Metropolitan Statistical Area. The City may allow deductions from the total family wage by employers who demonstrate one or more basic needs are covered elsewhere in a worker's compensation package. If the City of Spokane does not calculate a family wage, then eligible employers must provide, at minimum, a wage equal to the higher of either (1) three times the federal poverty guidelines for a family of two, or (2) any family wage rate previously calculated by the City of Spokane.

4.   The number of "full-time equivalent workers" equals the total number of hours an employer has paid its workers in a year divided by 2,080.

5.   "Worker" means an individual employed on a full-time, part-time, temporary, or seasonal basis, including independent contractors, contracted workers, contingent workers, and persons made available to work for the employer through the services of a temporary service, staffing, employment agency, or similar entity. The rights in this section extend to all workers who are physically-present in Spokane for any portion of the worker's employment.

C.   Enforcement

1.   Any worker, government entity, or nonprofit entity, may bring an action against the worker's employer for violation of these rights, and is entitled to attorney fees and costs in addition to legal remedies, including back pay, and equitable remedies, including reinstatement. Employers are not entitled to attorney fees and costs under this section.

2.   Any person may bring an action against the City of Spokane for failure to promulgate rules and policies necessary for enabling and effectuating the Right to a Family Wage, and that person shall be entitled to attorney fees and costs, in addition to equitable remedies. No action shall lie against the City for failure to enforce the rights contained within this section.

Section 2. Effective Date and Implementation of Rights

If approved by the electors, this section shall take effect and be in full force one year from the issuance of the certificate of election by the Spokane County Auditor's Office, except:

Employers shall be required to fully comply with the requirements of the Family Wage Right two years from the effective date, but shall only be required to pay at least 60% of the required wage on the effective date, and 80% of the required wage one year from the effective date.

Section 3. Repealer, Interpretation, and Severability

All ordinances, resolutions, motions, or orders in conflict with this section are hereby repealed to the extent of such conflict. The people of Spokane intend for this section to be liberally interpreted to effectuate the broad policy goals articulated in the preamble to the charter amendments set forth in Initiative No. 2015-2, and to be self-executing. If any part or provision of these section provisions is held invalid, the remainder of these provisions shall not be affected by such a holding and shall continue in full force and effect.

City of Lafayette Charter (Colorado)

Section 2.3. – Community Bill of Rights and obligations—The protection of these rights by prohibiting natural gas and oil extraction.

The rights secured here are not mere privileges; they are obligations justly placed on government and on each member of the community to respect freedoms held individually and collectively by every member of the community. The protection of these rights constitutes the highest and best use of the police powers that this municipality possesses.

Throughout this Section, the term "ecosystem" shall include, but not be limited to, air, soil, independent (non-corporate centrally controlled or contracted) agriculture, naturally occurring plants, animals, wetlands, streams, rivers, aquifers, and other water systems.

All rights secured by this Charter and this Section shall be self-executing. These rights shall be enforceable against private and public entities. The rights specifically enumerated by this Community Bill of Rights Section are enforceable exclusively with regard to the extraction of natural gas and oil, as prohibited by this charter provision. The expansion of protections of the rights herein enumerated, and the further enumeration of rights, as well as additional prohibitions against rights-denying behavior, through citizen use of the initiative process, is hereby encouraged. The Community Bill of Rights and Obligations is law, as follows:

a.   Right to community self-government. All residents of the City of Lafayette possess the fundamental and unalienable right to a form of governance where they live which recognizes that all power is inherent in the people, that all free governments are founded on the people's authority and consent, and that corporate entities and their directors and managers shall not enjoy special privileges or powers under the law which make community majorities subordinate to them.

b.   People as sovereign. The City of Lafayette shall be the governing authority responsible to, and governed by, the residents of the City. Use of the "City of Lafayette" municipal corporation by the sovereign people of the City to make law shall not be construed to limit or surrender the sovereign authority or immunities of the people to a municipal corporation that is subordinate to them in all respects at all times. The people at all times enjoy and retain an unalienable and indefeasible right to self-governance in the community where they reside.

c.   Right to clean water. All residents and ecosystems in the City of Lafayette possess a fundamental and unalienable right to sustainably access, use, consume, and preserve water drawn from natural water cycles that provide water necessary to sustain life—free from toxins, carcinogens, particulates, nucleotides, hydrocarbons and other substances introduced into the environment.

d. Right to clean air. All residents and ecosystems in the City of Lafayette possess a fundamental and unalienable right to breathe air untainted by toxins, carcinogens, particulates, nucleotides, hydrocarbons and other substances introduced into the environment.

e. Right to be free from chemical trespass. All residents and ecosystems within the City of Lafayette possess a fundamental and unalienable right to be free from involuntary chemical trespass including toxins, carcinogens, particulates, nucleotides, hydrocarbons and other substances introduced into the environment.

f. Right to peaceful enjoyment of home. Residents of the City of Lafayette possess a fundamental and unalienable right to the peaceful enjoyment of their homes, free from interference, intrusion, nuisances or impediments to access and occupation.

g. Rights of ecosystems. Ecosystems possess unalienable and fundamental rights to exist and flourish within the City of Lafayette. Residents of the City shall possess legal standing to enforce those rights on behalf of those ecosystems.

h. Right to a sustainable energy future. All residents in the City of Lafayette possess a right to a sustainable, healthy energy future, which includes, but is not limited to, the development, production, and use of energy from renewable, healthy, and sustainable fuel sources, exclusive of fossil and nuclear fuels, and the right to establish local sustainable energy policies to further secure this right.

i. Securing and protecting rights. To further secure and protect the rights enumerated by the Community Bill of Rights:

1. It shall be unlawful for any corporation or any person using a corporation to engage in the extraction of gas or oil within the City of Lafayette, with the exception of wells active and producing at the time this Charter Provision is enacted, and with the restriction and prohibition against the activation of inactive wells and the prohibition against the use of extraction technologies not in use in existing and producing wells at the time of enactment of this Charter provision.

2. It shall be unlawful for any corporation or any person using a corporation to deposit, store or transport waste water, "produced" water, "frack" water, brine or other materials, chemicals or by-products used in or resulting from the extraction of gas or oil, within, upon or through the land, air or waters of the City of Lafayette.

3. It shall be unlawful for any corporation, or person using a corporation, to engage in the creation of fossil fuel, nuclear

or other non-sustainable energy production and delivery infrastructures, such as pipelines, processing facilities, compressors, or storage and transportation facilities that support or facilitate industrial activities related to the extraction of natural gas and oil.

4. It shall be unlawful for any corporation or person using a corporation to extract water from surface or sub-surface sources in the City of Lafayette for use in the extraction of gas or oil.

5. Corporations and persons using corporations to engage in gas or oil extraction in a neighboring municipality, county or state shall be strictly liable for all harms caused to natural water sources, ecosystems, people and human communities within the City of Lafayette.

6. Corporations in violation of the prohibition against gas and oil extraction, or seeking to engage in gas or oil extraction shall not have the rights of "persons" afforded by the United States and Colorado constitutions, nor shall those corporations be afforded the protections of the commerce or contracts clauses within the United States Constitution or corresponding sections of the Colorado Constitution.

7. Corporations engaged in the extraction of gas or oil shall not possess the authority or power to enforce State or federal preemptive law against the people of the City of Lafayette, or to challenge or overturn municipal ordinances or Charter provisions.

8. No permit, license, privilege or charter issued by any State or federal agency, Commission or Board to any person or any corporation operating under a State charter, or any director, officer, owner, or manager of a corporation operating under a State charter, which would violate the prohibitions of this Charter provision or deprive any City resident(s) or ecosystem of any rights, privileges, or immunities secured by this Charter, the Colorado Constitution, the United States Constitution, or other laws, shall be deemed valid within the City of Lafayette.

9. Any person, corporation, or other entity that violates any prohibition of this Ordinance shall be guilty of a summary offense and, upon conviction, shall be sentenced to pay the maximum fine allowable under State law for that violation, and shall be subject to imprisonment to the extent allowed by law. A separate offense shall arise for each day or portion thereof in which a violation occurs and for each section of this Ordinance found to be violated. Enforcement of this article

      may be initiated by the Lafayette Police Department, the Director of Public Safety, or other designee of City Council. Lafayette may also enforce this Ordinance through an action in equity. In such an action, Lafayette shall be entitled to recover damages and all costs of litigation, including, without limitation, expert and attorney's fees.

10.   Any City resident shall have the authority to enforce this Ordinance through an action in equity. In such an action, the resident shall be entitled to recover damages and all costs of litigation, including, without limitation, expert and attorney's fees. Any person who brings an action to secure or protect the rights of ecosystems within Lafayette shall bring that action in the name of the ecosystem in a court of competent jurisdiction. Damages shall be measured by the cost of restoring the ecosystem to its pre-damaged state, and shall be paid to Lafayette or other applicable governmental entity, to be used exclusively for the full and complete restoration of the ecosystem.

11.   The provisions of this section are severable. If any court of competent jurisdiction decides that any sub-section, clause, sentence, part, or provision of this section is illegal, invalid, or unconstitutional, such decision shall not affect, impair, or invalidate any of the remaining sub-sections, clauses, sentences, parts, or provisions of this Community Bill of Rights and its prohibitions. The People of the City of Lafayette hereby declare that in the event of such a decision, and the determination that the court's ruling is legitimate, they would have enacted this amendment even without the sub-section, clause, sentence, part, or provision that the court decides is illegal, invalid, or unconstitutional.

(Approved at election held Nov. 5, 2013)

An Ordinance of Benton County, Oregon
A Food Bill of Rights

Whereas, a sustainable food system within Benton County is essential to the well-being of the County's residents, natural communities, living soils, and ecosystems, as well as the health and flourishing of the local economy, of which agriculture plays a vital role;

Whereas, sustainable food systems are those that do not harm the right of natural communities and ecosystems to exist, persist, and flourish, that promote biodiversity, resilience, and productivity, and that provide for the social, equitable, nutritional, economic, and cultural enhancement of the quality of life in Benton County;

Whereas, the practice of saving seeds of a harvested crop, especially heritage seed developed over the millennia and bequeathed from one generation to another, is fundamental to biodiversity, resilience, and a sustainable food system. Contamination or threat of contamination by genetically modified organisms (GMO's) is irreversible and can cause the extinction of seed varieties long held as common property by the people and the farmers and growers who developed them;

Whereas, the harvesting and saving of seed for replanting for another generation is the very foundation of a sustainable food system;

Whereas, the patenting, genetic alteration, and ownership of seeds that consequently contaminate conventional and organic crops grown in Benton County is antithetical to a sustainable food system. Involuntary contamination of crops results in growers' inability to harvest or replant their own seed, and loss of revenue from sale to markets that refuse to accept GMO-contaminated and trans-genetic risk seed products. It also results in litigation costs that must be borne by the grower against those holding GMO seed patents; all of which threatens the economic viability of Benton County farmers and growers;

Whereas, unsustainable farming practices pose significant threats to the health, safety, and welfare of residents, natural communities, and ecosystems within Benton County, and those practices violate the right of the people of Benton County to a sustainable food system;

Whereas, genetically engineered life forms and genetically modified organisms pose a significant risk to the health and well-being of the residents, natural communities, and ecosystems—including living soils, water, and air—within Benton County;

Whereas, the farming of genetically modified organisms, and the associated increased use of herbicides and pesticides that disrupt natural soil fertility and bioactivity, pose significant risks to sustainable food systems through irreversible alteration and contamination of soil life forms and the natural ecology of living soil systems;

Whereas, genetically modified life forms pose significant risks to sustainable food systems through irreversible contamination of crops and related species due to pollen drift; dispersal by insects, birds, rodents; and accidental spills from combines, trucks, and processing facilities; and genetically modified life forms have crossed with crops and weeds of similar species;

Whereas, the farming of genetically modified organisms poses a significant threat to nearby farmers' ability to attain or retain organic certification, and to sell either conventional or organic crops where genetically engineered contamination is prohibited, while previous farming practices without genetically engineered crops pose no such threats; thus conventional and organic crops cannot co-exist with genetically engineered crops of the same or similar species without causing harm to a sustainable food system, seed heritage and/or the economic viability of organic or conventional farm operations;

Whereas, the people of Benton County understand that meaningful lawmaking which curtails the authority of agribusiness corporations to engage in unsustainable farming practices—such as obtaining patents on genetically engineered living processes and organisms like seeds—may run afoul of claimed corporate rights or powers. And the people understand further that those rights and powers are routinely used to usurp the rights of people, their communities, natural communities, and ecosystems and thus prevent people from addressing local concerns, such as sustainable food systems and seed heritage; and the people understand further that such rights and powers include the ability to wield licenses, the constitutional rights of persons, and the legal doctrine of preemption to strike local ordinances that weigh the pertinent health, safety, and welfare concerns differently from how they are weighed by other levels of government; and

Whereas, this Ordinance is enacted pursuant to the inherent and inalienable right of the residents of Benton County to govern their own county, including, without limitation, as secured by the Declaration of Independence's assertion that governments are instituted to secure the rights of people, in the State Constitution of Oregon's recognition that all power is inherent in the people, and in the Benton County Charter, which delegates the authority to the people and their representatives to enact local legislation on matters of county concern;

Therefore, the people of Benton County do ordain, through this Ordinance, which shall be known and cited as the Benton County Food Bill of Rights Ordinance.

Section 1. Findings and Intent

The people of Benton County declare that we possess the right to community self-government and that our right to local self-governance is a fundamental and inalienable right. We assert that right to adopt this ordinance, which creates a food bill of rights for the people of the County, and which protects seed heritage. We find that corporate involvement in agriculture interferes with our right to local self-government, given the ability of corporations to use their wealth and power to determine agricultural policy. Those corporate agricultural policies include laws and regulations which permit genetic engineering and genetic modification of life forms and organisms, and which allow the use of such life forms and organisms.

Accordingly, the people of Benton County adopt this ordinance, which prohibits corporations from engaging in the planting, growing, cultivating, raising, harvesting, or processing of genetically engineered life forms or genetically modified organisms. To effectuate these prohibitions, the people of Benton County have determined that we must elevate our right to community self-government above the "rights" claimed by corporations; otherwise our right to local self-governance shall be forever subordinated to governance by a corporate few, which is not a democracy.

Section 2. Authority
This Ordinance is enacted pursuant to the inherent right of the residents of Benton County to govern their own county, as recognized by authorities including, without limitation, the Declaration of Independence's assertion that governments are instituted to secure the rights of people; Section 1 of the Oregon Constitution which recognizes that "all power is inherent in the people"; Article VI, Section 10 of the Oregon Constitution which guarantees home rule powers to Counties; and Section 203.035 of Chapter 203 of the Oregon Revised Statutes, which grants counties ordinance-making power to address matters of county concern.

Section 3. Definitions

(a)   "Corporation": Shall refer to any corporation, limited partnership, limited liability partnership, business trust, or limited liability corporation organized under the laws of any State of the United States or under the laws of any country, and any other business entity that possesses government-conferred limited liability attributes for its owners, directors, officers, and /or managers.

(b)   "Food": All things edible that are locally grown, raised, harvested, collected, prepared, or processed for consumption.

(c)   "Genetically Engineered Organism" or "Genetically Modified Life Form": Any organism or organisms in which the genetic material has been changed through the application of:

(1)   In vitro nucleic acid techniques, including recombinant deoxyribonucleic acid (DNA) techniques and the direct injection of nucleic acid into cells or organelles, or

(2)   Fusion of cells (including protoplast fusion) or hybridization techniques that overcome natural physiological, reproductive, or recombination barriers, where the donor cells/protoplasts do not fall within the same taxonomic family, in a way that does not occur by natural multiplication or natural recombination.

The phrase shall also include all equivalent terms, and may interchangeably be referred to as "GMO's" or "genetically engineered" or "genetically modified" life forms. The phrase shall not include traditional selective breeding, conjugation, fermentation, hybridization, in vitro fertilization, or tissue culture.

(d)   "In vitro nucleic acid techniques": This phrase shall include, but not be not limited to, recombinant DNA or RNA techniques that use vector systems and techniques involving the direct introduction into the organisms of hereditary materials prepared outside the organisms such as micro-injection, macro-injection, chemoporation, electroporation, microencapsulation, and liposome fusion.

(e)   "Living Soils": Biologically and chemically resilient, balanced communities of bacteria, fungi, protozoa, nematodes, worms, and other soil organisms, cycling minerals necessary for a nutritionally dense food system. The phrase shall not include any soils that contain Genetically Modified Organisms or accompanying pesticides.

(f)   "Locally Grown, Raised, Harvested, Collected, Prepared, or Processed": The phrase shall include, but not be limited to, all foods grown, raised, harvested, collected, prepared, or processed within Benton County.

(g)   "Organism": Any biological entity capable of replication, reproduction, or transferring genetic material, exclusive of human beings and human fetuses. The term organism shall include seeds.

(h)   "Seed Heritage": Seeds inherited from family or community, generation after generation, carefully stewarded by the inheritors so they can be passed to future generations, are adapted to the local climate, are held in the commons, usually by a family or community, or by seed growers that specialize in open-pollinated and heritage seed.

(i)   "Sustainable Agriculture": Agriculture conducted pursuant to the provisions of U.S. Code Title 7, Section 3103.19 which does not violate the rights of natural communities and ecosystems as recognized by this Ordinance; which respects the inalienable right to Sustainable Food Systems and Seed Heritage; which provides a viable income for farming and harvesting families; which meets all applicable state and federal pollution control requirements for farming and food processing practices; which maintains plants, soil, air, water, and animals free from genetic modifications; which is free from the application of sewage sludge as well as urban and industrial waste not properly composted; and that provides for the humane treatment of livestock.

(j)   "Sustainable Food System": A food system that recognizes the rights of the people to sustainable agriculture, to seed heritage, and to biologically resilient living soils, while not violating the right of natural communities and ecosystems to exist, persist, and flourish, and which promotes biodiversity, resilience, and nutrient density while providing for the social, equitable, economic, nutritional and cultural enhancements of the quality of life in Benton County.

(k)   "Trans genetic risk": A crop including, but not limited to, corn, soy, flax, canola, wheat, and beets that have been genetically modified, making all seeds of those crops and related crops subject to traces of that alteration.

Section 4. Food Bill of Rights

(a)   *Right to Sustainable Food Systems*: All residents of Benton County possess the fundamental and inalienable right to access, use, consume, produce, harvest, collect, process, and distribute foods generated from sustainable agriculture and sustainable food systems. This right shall include the right to be free from unsustainable food systems and unsustainable agricultural practices, which interfere with the right of Benton County residents to a sustainable food system.

(b)   *Right to Seed Heritage*: All residents of Benton County possess the inalienable right to save, preserve, protect, collect, harvest, and distribute all seeds grown within Benton County as essential to maintaining a sustainable food system. This includes, but is not limited to, the right to be free from infection, infestation, or drift by any means from genetically engineered life forms or genetically modified organisms.

(c)   *Rights of Natural Communities*: Natural communities and ecosystems within Benton County, including living soils and other terrestrial systems and aquatic systems such as aquifers, streams, rivers, and wetlands, and the systems of life that inhabit them, possess inalienable and fundamental rights to exist, persist, maintain themselves, and regenerate their own vital cycles, structure, functions, and evolutionary processes within Benton County. Natural communities and ecosystems possess an inalienable right to be free from the patenting or ownership of their genetic essence. Residents of Benton County shall possess legal standing to enforce these rights of natural communities and ecosystems, regardless of their relationship to them as property.

(d)   *Right to Self-Government*: All residents of Benton County possess the fundamental and inalienable right to a form of governance where they live which recognizes that all power is inherent in the people, that all free governments are founded on the people's authority and consent, and that corporate entities and their directors and managers shall not enjoy special privileges or powers under the law which make community majorities subordinate to them.

(e)   *People are Sovereign*: Benton County shall be the governing authority responsible to, and governed by, the residents of Benton County. Use of the Benton County municipal corporation by the sovereign people of Benton County to make law shall not be construed to limit or surrender the sovereign authority or immunities of the people to a municipal corporation that is subordinate to them in all respects at all times. The people at all times enjoy and retain an inalienable and indefeasible right to self-governance in the community where they reside.

(f)   *Rights are Self-Executing*: All rights delineated and secured by this ordinance shall be self-executing, and these rights shall be enforceable against both public and private actors, and shall not require implementing legislation for their enforceability.

Section 5. Prohibitions Necessary to Secure the Food Bill of Rights

(a)   It shall be unlawful for any corporation or governmental entity to engage in the planting, growing, cultivating, raising, rearing, or harvesting of genetically engineered life forms or genetically modified organisms within Benton County. The phrase "engage in" shall include, but not be limited to, the sale and/or patenting of the genetically engineered life form or genetically modified organism, which is used for planting, growing, cultivating, raising, rearing, or harvesting within Benton County.

(b)   No resident, farmer, or locally owned business within Benton County shall be liable to any corporation claiming loss of income or commercial infringement resulting from the inadvertent infection of agricultural crops by genetically engineered life forms or genetically modified organisms.

(c)   No permit, license, privilege, or charter issued by any State or federal agency, International Body, Commission, or Board to any person or any corporation operating under a State charter, or any director, officer, owner, or manager of a corporation operating under a State charter, which would violate the prohibitions of this Ordinance or deprive any resident(s), natural community, or ecosystem within Benton County of any rights, privileges, or immunities secured by this Ordinance, the Oregon Constitution, the United States Constitution, or other laws, shall be deemed valid within Benton County.

(d)   Corporations engaged in the planting, growing, cultivating, raising, rearing, or harvesting of genetically engineered life forms or genetically modified organisms in any municipality adjacent to Benton County whose activities result in genetically modified organisms entering Benton County shall be strictly liable for damages caused by that entry, including, but not limited to, any loss of income or commercial infringement.

Section 6. Implementation

(a)   Existing, non-perennial genetically modified organisms and genetically engineered life forms within Benton County must be harvested, or removed from Benton County, within six months after the effective date of this Ordinance.

(b)   Existing, perennial genetically modified organisms and genetically engineered life forms within Benton County must be destroyed within six months of the effective date of this Ordinance.

(c)   Six (6) months after the effective date of this Ordinance, owners of patents of genetically modified organisms and genetically engineered life forms which exist within the County on lands owned by residents, corporations, or governmental entities, where the genetically modified organism or life form was not intentionally put there by the land owner, shall be liable for the costs of clean-up and removal, and the costs of contamination of lands, seeds, or organisms owned by residents, corporations, or governmental entities within the County.

(d)   Any trans genetic risk seed must be tested by a reputable lab prior to planting in Benton County to show that it is free of traces of genetic modification, and these tests must be available to the public.

Section 7. Enforcement

(a)   Benton County may enforce this Ordinance through an action brought in a court of competent jurisdiction. In such an action, Benton County shall be entitled to recover all costs of litigation, including, without limitation, expert and attorney's fees. Violation of the prohibitions established by this Ordinance shall also be a criminal offense, and action against the violator shall be brought by the County in a court of competent jurisdiction.

(b)   For three years following enactment of this Ordinance, all locations where genetically modified organisms and genetically engineered life forms have been grown, processed, or stored must be monitored by landowners for volunteer seedlings, re-growth of forage sod, stump sprouting, or perennials such as alfalfa. Fines established by Benton County shall be imposed on landowners for allowing re-growth of genetically modified organisms and genetically engineered life forms on lands formerly and intentionally planted with them. Cross-pollination or contamination of non-genetically modified organisms or non-genetically engineered life forms from re-established genetically modified organisms and genetically engineered life forms shall be cause for penalty and restitution.

(c)   Any resident or group of residents within Benton County shall have legal standing and the authority to enforce the provisions of this Ordinance in a court of competent jurisdiction. In such an action, the resident or group of residents shall be entitled to recover damages and all costs of litigation, including, without limitation, expert and attorney's fees.

(d)   Any action brought to remedy the violation of the rights of natural communities or ecosystems shall list the natural community or ecosystem as a plaintiff in the action, damages sought must bear a relationship to the damage inflicted upon the natural community or ecosystem, and awarded damages must be payable to the municipality for the restricted use of repairing the natural community or ecosystem.

(e)   Corporations engaged in activities prohibited by this Ordinance, or seeking to engage in activities that would violate the prohibitions of this Ordinance, shall not have the rights of "persons" nor access to legal protections afforded to persons by the United States and Oregon Constitutions, nor shall those corporations be afforded rights under the 1st or 5th or 11th amendments to the United States Constitution or corresponding sections of the Oregon Constitution, nor shall those corporations be afforded the protections of the Commerce or Contracts clauses within the United States Constitution or corresponding sections of the Oregon Constitution.

(f)   Corporations engaged in activities prohibited by this Ordinance, or seeking to engage in activities that would violate the prohibitions of this Ordinance, shall not possess the authority or power to enforce federal or state preemptive law against the people of Benton County, or to challenge or overturn this Ordinance, or any rules or regulations implemented to enforce this Ordinance, when that enforcement or challenge interferes with the rights asserted by this Ordinance or interferes with the authority of Benton County to protect the health, safety, and welfare of its residents.

Section 8. People's Right to Self-Government

The foundation for the making and adoption of this Ordinance is the people's fundamental and inalienable right to govern themselves, and thereby secure their rights to life, liberty, and the pursuit of happiness. Any attempts to use other units and levels of government to preempt, amend, alter, or overturn this Ordinance, or parts of this Ordinance, shall require Benton County to hold public hearings that explore the adoption of other measures that expand the ability of residents to protect their fundamental and inalienable right to self-government, including without limitation, the amendment of the Benton County Charter.

Section 9. Oregon Constitutional Changes

Through the adoption of this ordinance, the people of Benton County call for state recognition of municipal food bills of rights. Accordingly, the people of Benton County call for changes to be made to the Oregon Constitution which recognize and secure a community right to local self-government that cannot be preempted by the State if the community's laws enforce standards and rights more protective of the health, safety, and welfare of the people of Benton County and the natural environment. The people of the County also call for state constitutional changes that elevate community rights above those claimed by corporations when community rights conflict with corporate privileges, and that recognize the rights of nature enforceable by the residents of a community.

Section 10. Severability

The provisions of this Ordinance are severable. If any court of competent jurisdiction decides that any section, clause, sentence, part, or provision of this Ordinance is illegal, invalid, or unconstitutional, such decision shall not affect, impair, or invalidate any of the remaining sections, clauses, sentences, parts, or provisions of this Ordinance. The people of Benton County hereby declare that in the event of such a decision, and the determination that the court's ruling is legitimate, it would have enacted this Ordinance even without the section, clause, sentence, part, or provision that the court decides is illegal, invalid, or unconstitutional.

Section 11. Repealer

All inconsistent provisions within the county code of Benton County are hereby repealed, but only to the extent necessary to remedy the inconsistency.

Section 12. Effect

This Ordinance shall take effect 90 days after adoption.

Broadview Heights Community Bill of Rights (Ohio)

a. Right to Pure Water. All residents, natural communities and ecosystems in The City of Broadview Heights possess a fundamental and inalienable right to sustainably access, use, consume, and preserve water drawn from natural water cycles that provide water necessary to sustain life within the City.

b. Right to Clean Air. All residents, natural communities and ecosystems in The City of Broadview Heights possess a fundamental and inalienable right to breathe air untainted by toxins, carcinogens, particulates and other substances known to cause harm to health.

c. Right to Peaceful Enjoyment of Home. Residents of The City of Broadview Heights possess a fundamental and inalienable right to the peaceful enjoyment of their homes, free from interference, intrusion, nuisances or impediments to access and occupation.

d. Rights of Natural Communities. Natural communities and ecosystems, including, but not limited to, wetlands, streams, rivers, aquifers, and other water systems possess inalienable and fundamental rights to exist and flourish within The City of Broadview Heights. Residents of the City shall possess legal standing to enforce those rights on behalf of those natural communities and ecosystems.

e. Right to a Sustainable Energy Future. All residents in The City of Broadview Heights possess a right to a sustainable energy future, which includes, but is not limited to, the development, production, and use of energy from renewable and sustainable fuel sources.

f. Right to Self-Government. All residents of The City of Broadview Heights possess the fundamental and inalienable right to a form of governance where they live which recognizes that all power is inherent in the people, that all free governments are founded on the people's authority and consent, and that corporate entities and their directors and managers shall not enjoy special privileges or powers under the law which make community majorities subordinate to them.

g. People as Sovereign. The City of Broadview Heights shall be the governing authority responsible to, and governed by, the residents of the City. Use of the "City of Broadview Heights" municipal corporation by the sovereign people of the City to make law shall not be construed to limit or surrender the sovereign authority or immunities of the people to a municipal corporation that is subordinate to them in all respects at all times. The people at all times enjoy and retain an inalienable and indefeasible right to self-governance in the community where they reside.

h.   Rights as Self-Executing. All rights delineated and secured by this Charter shall be self-executing and these rights shall be enforceable against private and public entities.

i.   Securing and Protecting Rights. To further secure and protect the rights enumerated by the Bill of Rights:

1. It shall be unlawful for any person or corporation to engage in the extraction of gas or oil within The City of Broadview Heights, with the exception of gas and oil wells installed and operating at the time of enactment of this Charter provision, provided that the extraction of gas or oil from those existing wells does not involve any practice or process not previously used for the extraction of gas or oil from those wells and providing those wells are capped securely when production ceases

2. It shall be unlawful for any person or corporation, or any director, officer, owner, or manager of a corporation to use a corporation, to deposit, store or transport waste water, "produced" water, "frack" water, brine or other materials, chemicals or by-products used in the extraction of gas or oil, within, upon or through the land, air or waters of The City of Broadview Heights.

3. It shall be unlawful for any person or corporation, or any director, officer, owner, or manager of a corporation to use a corporation, to engage in the creation of fossil fuel, nuclear or other non-sustainable energy production and delivery infrastructures, such as pipelines, processing facilities, compressors, or storage and transportation facilities of any sort that would violate the right to a sustainable energy future for The City of Broadview Heights.

4. Corporations and persons using corporations to engage in gas or oil extraction in a neighboring municipality, county or state shall be strictly liable for all harms caused to natural water sources, ecosystems, human and natural communities within The City of Broadview Heights.

5. Corporations in violation of the prohibition against gas and oil extraction, or seeking to engage in gas or oil extraction shall not have the rights of "persons" afforded by the United States and Ohio Constitutions, nor shall those corporations be afforded the protections of the commerce or contracts clauses within the United States Constitution or corresponding sections of the Ohio Constitution.

6. Corporations engaged in the extraction of gas or oil shall not possess the authority or power to enforce State or federal

preemptive law against the people of The City of Broadview Heights, or to challenge or overturn municipal ordinances or Charter provisions adopted by The City of Broadview Heights Council.

7. No permit, license, privilege or charter issued by any State or federal agency, Commission or Board to any person or any corporation operating under a State charter, or any director, officer, owner, or manager of a corporation operating under a State charter, which would violate the prohibitions of this Charter provision or deprive any City resident(s), natural community, or ecosystem of any rights, privileges, or immunities secured by this Charter, the Ohio Constitution, the United States Constitution, or other laws, shall be deemed valid within The City of Broadview Heights.

8. Any person, corporation, or other entity that violates any prohibition of this Ordinance shall be guilty of a summary offense and, upon conviction shall be sentenced to pay the maximum fine allowable under State law for that violation, and shall be imprisoned to the extent allowed by law. A separate offense shall arise for each day or portion thereof in which a violation occurs and for each section of this Ordinance found to be violated. Enforcement of this article may be initiated by the Broadview Heights Police Department, the Director of Public Safety, or other designee of City Council. Broadview Heights may also enforce this Ordinance through an action in equity. In such an action, Broadview Heights shall be entitled to recover damages and all costs of litigation, including, without limitation, expert and attorney's fees.

9. Any City resident shall have the authority to enforce this Ordinance through an action in equity. In such an action, the resident shall be entitled to recover damages and all costs of litigation, including, without limitation, expert and attorney's fees. Any person who brings an action to secure or protect the rights of natural communities or ecosystems within Broadview Heights shall bring that action in the name of the natural community or ecosystem in a court of competent jurisdiction. Damages shall be measured by the cost of restoring the natural community or ecosystem to its pre-damaged state, and shall be paid to Broadview Heights or other applicable governmental entity, to be used exclusively for the full and complete restoration of the natural community or ecosystem.

10. The provisions of this section are severable. If any court of competent jurisdiction decides that any sub-section, clause,

sentence, part, or provision of this section is illegal, invalid, or unconstitutional, such decision shall not affect, impair, or invalidate any of the remaining sub-sections, clauses, sentences, parts, or provisions of this Bill of Rights and its prohibitions. The People of The City of Broadview Heights hereby declare that in the event of such a decision, and the determination that the court's ruling is legitimate, they would have enacted this amendment even without the sub-section, clause, sentence, part, or provision that the court decides is illegal, invalid, or unconstitutional. All inconsistent provisions of prior Ordinances and zoning Ordinances adopted at any time by The City of Broadview Heights are hereby held in abeyance, but shall take immediate effect in the event this Bill of Rights and its protective prohibitions are overturned.

About the Authors

THOMAS LINZEY IS AN ATTORNEY AND the executive director of the Community Environmental Legal Defense Fund, a nonprofit law firm that has provided assistance to over five hundred municipal governments and nonprofit organizations in the United States. He is the coauthor of *YES!* magazine's *This Changes Everything.*

ANNEKE CAMPBELL IS A WRITER AND documentary filmmaker who has worked for many years to advance the causes of justice and respect for all humanity and the environment. She is the coauthor of *Moonrise: The Power of Women Leading from the Heart.*

PM Press was founded at the end of 2007 by a small collection of folks with decades of publishing, media, and organizing experience. PM Press co-conspirators have published and distributed hundreds of books, pamphlets, CDs, and DVDs. Members of PM have founded enduring book fairs, spearheaded victorious tenant organizing campaigns, and worked closely with bookstores, academic conferences, and even rock bands to deliver political and challenging ideas to all walks of life. We're old enough to know what we're doing and young enough to know what's at stake.

We seek to create radical and stimulating fiction and non-fiction books, pamphlets, T-shirts, visual and audio materials to entertain, educate, and inspire you. We aim to distribute these through every available channel with every available technology—whether that means you are seeing anarchist classics at our bookfair stalls; reading our latest vegan cookbook at the café; downloading geeky fiction e-books; or digging new music and timely videos from our website.

PM Press is always on the lookout for talented and skilled volunteers, artists, activists, and writers to work with. If you have a great idea for a project or can contribute in some way, please get in touch.

PM Press
PO Box 23912
Oakland CA 94623
510-658-3906
www.pmpress.org

FRIENDS OF PM

These are indisputably momentous times—the financial system is melting down globally and the Empire is stumbling. Now more than ever there is a vital need for radical ideas.

In the many years since its founding—and on a mere shoestring—PM Press has risen to the formidable challenge of publishing and distributing knowledge and entertainment for the struggles ahead. With hundreds of releases to date, we have published an impressive and stimulating array of literature, art, music, politics, and culture. Using every available medium, we've succeeded in connecting those hungry for ideas and information to those putting them into practice.

Friends of PM allows you to directly help impact, amplify, and revitalize the discourse and actions of radical writers, filmmakers, and artists. It provides us with a stable foundation from which we can build upon our early successes and provides a much-needed subsidy for the materials that can't necessarily pay their own way. You can help make that happen—and receive every new title automatically delivered to your door once a month—by joining as a Friend of PM Press. And, we'll throw in a free T-shirt when you sign up.

Here are your options:
- $30 a month: Get all books and pamphlets plus 50% discount on all webstore purchases
- $40 a month: Get all PM Press releases (including CDs and DVDs) plus 50% discount on all webstore purchases
- $100 a month: Superstar—Everything plus PM merchandise, free downloads, and 50% discount on all webstore purchases

For those who can't afford $30 or more a month, we have Sustainer Rates at $15, $10, and $5. Sustainers get a free PM Press T-shirt and a 50% discount on all purchases from our website.

Your Visa or Mastercard will be billed once a month, until you tell us to stop. Or until our efforts succeed in bringing the revolution around. Or the financial meltdown of Capital makes plastic redundant. Whichever comes first.

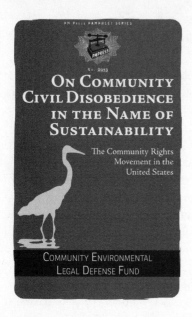

On Community Civil Disobedience in the Name of Sustainability
The Community Rights Movement in the United States
Community Environmental Legal Defense Fund
Introduction by Thomas Linzey
$6.95 • ISBN: 978-1-62963-126-4
8.5x5.5 • 64 pages

Humanity stands at the brink of global environmental and economic collapse. We have pinned our future to an economic system that centralizes power in fewer and fewer hands, and whose benefits increasingly flow to smaller and smaller numbers of people. Our system of government is similarly medieval—relying on a 1780s constitutional form of government written to guarantee the exploitation of the natural environment and elevate "the endless production of more" over the rights of people, nature, and their communities.

But right now, people within the community rights movement aren't waiting for power brokers to fix the system. They're beginning to envision a new sustainability constitution by adopting new laws at the local level that are forcing those ideas upward into the state and national ones. In doing so, they are directly challenging the basic operating system of this country— one which currently elevates corporate "rights" above the rights of people, nature, and their communities—and changing it into one which recognizes a right to local, community self-government that cannot be overridden by corporations, or by governments wielded by corporate interests.

This short primer from the Community Environmental Legal Defense Fund explores and describes the philosophy and underpinnings of the community rights movement that has emerged in the United States—a movement of nonviolent civil disobedience based on municipal lawmaking.

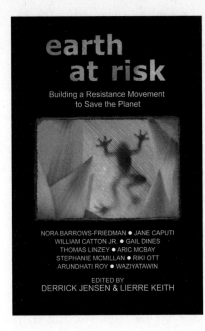

earth
at risk

Building a Resistance Movement
to Save the Planet

NORA BARROWS-FRIEDMAN ● JANE CAPUTI
WILLIAM CATTON JR. ● GAIL DINES
THOMAS LINZEY ● ARIC MCBAY
STEPHANIE MCMILLAN ● RIKI OTT
ARUNDHATI ROY ● WAZIYATAWIN
EDITED BY
DERRICK JENSEN & LIERRE KEITH

Earth at Risk
Building a Resistance Movement to Save the Planet
Edited by Derrick Jensen and Lierre Keith

$20.00 • ISBN: 978-1-60486-674-2
9x6 • 264 Pages

Industrial civilization is devouring the planet and the future. The oceans are acidifying, whole mountains have been laid to waste, and the climate is teetering into chaos. Every biome is approaching collapse. And fifty years of environmentalism hasn't even slowed the rate of destruction. Yet environmentalists are not considering strategies that might actually prevent the looming biocide we are facing.

Earth at Risk: Building a Resistance Movement to Save the Planet is an annual conference featuring environmental thinkers and activists who are willing to ask the hardest questions about the seriousness of our situation. The conference is convened by Derrick Jensen, acclaimed author of *Endgame*, who has argued that we need a resistance movement against civilization itself.

The twelve people in this volume present an impassioned critique of the dominant culture from every angle: William Catton Jr. explains ecological overshoot; Thomas Linzey gives a fiery call for community sovereignty; Jane Caputi exposes patriarchy's mythic dismemberment of the Goddess; Aric McBay discusses historically effective resistance strategies; and Stephanie McMillan takes down capitalism. One by one, they build an unassailable case that we need to deprive the rich of their ability to steal from the poor and the powerful of their ability to destroy the planet. These speakers offer their ideas on what can be done to build a real resistance movement, one that includes all levels of direct action—action that can actually match the scale of the problem.

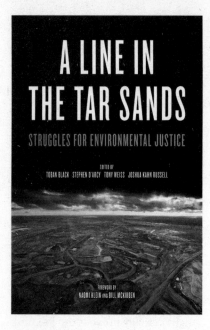

A Line in the Tar Sands

Struggles for Environmental Justice

Edited by Joshua Kahn Russell, Stephen D'Arcy, Tony Weis, and Toban Black
Foreword by Naomi Klein and Bill McKibben
$24.95 • ISBN: 978-1-62963-039-7
9x6 • 392 pages

The fight over the tar sands in North America is among the epic environmental and social justice battles of our time, and one of the first that has managed to quite explicitly marry concern for frontline communities and immediate local hazards with fear for the future of the entire planet.

Tar sands "development" comes with an enormous environmental and human cost. But tar sands opponents—fighting a powerful international industry—are likened to terrorists, government environmental scientists are muzzled, and public hearings are concealed and rushed.

Yet, despite the formidable political and economic power behind the tar sands, many opponents are actively building international networks of resistance, challenging pipeline plans while resisting threats to Indigenous sovereignty and democratic participation. Including leading voices involved in the struggle against the tar sands, *A Line in the Tar Sands* offers a critical analysis of the impact of the tar sands and the challenges opponents face in their efforts to organize effective resistance.

Contributors include: Angela Carter, Bill McKibben, Brian Tokar, Christine Leclerc, Clayton Thomas-Muller, Crystal Lameman, Dave Vasey, Emily Coats, Eriel Deranger, Greg Albo, Jeremy Brecher, Jess Worth, Jesse Cardinal, Joshua Kahn Russell, Lilian Yap, Linda Capato, Macdonald Stainsby, Martin Lukacs, Matt Leonard, Melina Laboucan-Massimo, Naomi Klein, Rae Breaux, Randolph Haluza-DeLay, Rex Weyler, Ryan Katz-Rosene, Sâkihitowin Awâsis, Sonia Grant, Stephen D'Arcy, Toban Black, Tony Weis, Tyler McCreary, Winona LaDuke, and Yves Engler.

The editors' proceeds from this book will be donated to frontline grassroots environmental justice groups and campaigns.